sexual violence, survivorship and solidarity

AGNES TÖRÖK

Burning Eye

Burning Eye Books
Never Knowingly
Mainstream

Copyright © 2017 Agnes Török

The author asserts the moral right under the Copyright, Designs and Patents Act 1988 to be identified as the author of this work.

All rights reserved. No part of this publication may be reproduced, stored in a retrieval system, or transmitted, in any form or by any means without the prior written consent of the author, nor be otherwise circulated in any form of binding or cover other than that in which it is published and without a similar condition being imposed on the subsequent purchaser.

This edition published by Burning Eye Books 2017

www.burningeye.co.uk

@burningeyebooks

Burning Eye Books
15 West Hill, Portishead, BS20 6LG

ISBN 978 1 911570 18 9

We Need to Talk

sexual violence, survivorship and solidarity

Contents

Statistics 11
This Book 13
Content Warning 15

Why We Need to Talk: An Introduction of Sorts

This Is 21
The Only Poem That Matters 22
Hidden 23
Looking Back 24

Everyone: We Need To Talk

About Myths And Narratives
   This Is Not Poetry 30
   Myths About Rape 31
   The Roles We Are Cast 33
   Age Of Violence 36
   Not Your Story 37

About Sexual Violence And Gender-Based Violence
   Definitions 43
   Public Secret 44
   This Body Is A Home 46
   Coral Reef 48

About Rape Culture And Structural Sexual Violence
   My Trauma Is Political 53
   Rape As Risk 54
   Dew Drops 56
   We Are Arming Perpetrators 59

About Criminal (In)Justice, Police And Politics
   Witch Trials 65
   Fear Is A Physical Creature 66
   The Police 68
   Dangerous People 70

Victims And Survivors: We Need To Talk

About Surviving
- I Wish Someone Had Told Me — 79
- Unbreakable — 80
- How To Suffer — 81
- How To Survive — 82

About Fighting
- Dear Future Self — 87
- Having A Panic Attack — 87
- I Imagine Safety — 89
- Surface — 90
- Floating — 92
- Things I Know For Sure — 94

About Living Again
- Surprised — 99
- Provincialising Violence — 101
- Technicolor — 103
- I'll Save You A Seat — 104

About The Fight Still Ahead Of Us
- The Circle — 109
- A Revolution Of Sorts — 110
- The End Of The Tunnel — 112
- What Do We Do? — 114

Friends And Family: We Need To Talk

About Understanding
- Things I Did To Cope — 121
- Trust — 122
- The Bell (Jar) — 123
- Surviving — 124
- Psychological Abuse — 125
- An Ordinary Life — 126

About Your Role In All Of This
- The Jury — 131
- Everyone Else — 133
- Exorcism — 134
- Ten Things — 136

About Your Job From Now On
I Believe You	141
Listen	142
Life Or Death	144
Why They Call Us Survivors	146

Everyone: We Need To Talk To Each Other

Listening To Victims And Survivors
They Will Say	152
Our Stories	153
Abuse	155
Watching The Door	156
Why I Stayed	158
We Don't Cry Wolf	160

About Masculinity
You're So Vain	167
Why Do Rape Apologists Think Men Are Animals?	168
Of Monsters And Men	170
No One Is Born A Rapist	173

About Consent
State Of Emergency	179
Speak	184

About How To Reclaim The Internet
Did You Know	191
Autocorrect	193
Online Violence	194
Just A Click Away	196
#Reclaimtheinternet	198

Everyone: We Need To Start Doing

What's Next
- We Know Where We Stand — 209
- It's Time For The Rapists' Shift — 210
- The Future — 211
- "It Gets Better" — 214

The Final Chapter: How To Change Everything
- We Need To Talk — 218
- Self-Help To Revolt — 221
- This Movement — 223
- How To Change Everything — 227

Bonus Section
Victims And Survivors: We Need To Write

Why Write?
- Writing As Therapy — 235
- Why Write Poems — 236

Writing Exercises
- Rules For The Writing Exercises — 238
- How To Survive: — 239
- Letter To My Future Self Having A Rough Time: — 242
- What I Need Now: — 245
- Letter To My Younger Self: — 248
- Mapping Your Way Forward: — 251
- Imagining The Future: — 255
- Reclaiming The Story: — 258
- How To Change Everything: — 261

More To Do

More To Read
- Reading Tips For Everyone — 277
- Resources For Victims And Survivors And Their Friends And Family — 278
- Final Tips From The Author — 278
- Finally — 280

statistics

every 98 seconds
someone is raped

only six
out of every 1,000 rapists
end up in prison

WE NEED TO TALK.

this book

I've heard enough times
that I should not write this book
to know
it needs to be written

Content Warning

This book is about sexual violence and gender-based violence. About how to understand it. About how to support and listen to those who have been subjected to it. About how to end structural violence. About how to change everything.

As such, poems in this book may be triggering to you if you have experienced rape, abuse or hate crime.

Fellow victims and survivors of violence – there are chapters written especially for you. With you in mind. The parts of the book marked 'victims and survivors' are intended to be safe and non-triggering to read no matter where you are in your recovery. They focus on coping mechanisms, community and change.

Under 'More to Do', there are resources and listed support services for you to turn to. In the bonus section at the end, 'We Need to Write', there are writing exercises for you. These are part of an arts therapy approach to dealing with trauma, and contain tools for writing your own story, on your own terms, in your own time.

People who have not been targeted with gender-based violence: read closely. Learn. Think. Feel. Listen. The subjects between these pages are matters of life and death.

Try not to shy away from them. From us.

Because we need to talk.

Why We Need to Talk

An introduction of sorts

Welcome to the book! I am really glad you have made it here. We need a lot more people like you.

There are a million reasons why we need to talk about sexual violence and gender-based violence. Because the way we speak about violence – and about victims – is a huge part of the problem.

Because victims' and survivors' stories are rarely heard from our own mouths, from our own pens, on our own terms, in our own time.

Because the silence that surrounds sexual violence – the shame and victim-blaming – literally kills. Every day.

Statistically speaking, you know several victims of sexual violence and at least one rapist. That means that you can be either part of the problem of silence and inaction – or part of the solution of conversation, consent and change.

This is a first step towards understanding. Listening. And changing everything. And I am so glad you are on board.

With love and solidarity,

this is

this is
not everyone's story
it's not even all of mine

this is
a stretching out of hands
an opening of arms
a parting of lips
into both a snarl
and a smile

this is
a drop in the ocean
a voice in the silence
a reclaiming of stories

this is
the book I wish someone had given me
when I desperately needed it
so I decided
to write it
myself

the only poem that matters

if I could write just one poem about sexual violence
it would be this:

Always.
Believe.
The victim.

hidden

I hid my words
as I hid your bottles
buried beneath
the battlefield
of our bed
the debris
of my nightstand

was this book
waiting
to happen

looking back

I will think back on this time
and think
how much I made
created with my own bare hands
how much I dreamt

I will look back and marvel
at how I sewed a patchwork of gold
from broken thread and fractured memories
how trauma and hope
came to be intertwined
by the might of my pen
my proud spine
the tears I have shattered between these pages
in the spaces between these lines

I will look back and think
how lonely it is
to bear so many stories within you
and never be sure when the last handkerchief
the last magic trick
will be pulled from inside your chest

I will look back and think
how painful it is
how healing it is
how it completely restructures you
to choose to tell the truth to yourself
to choose to put it into words
to choose to share it with strangers

I will look back and think
great things
about this time

but right now
when looking back
means being turned to stone
right now
all I can think is

keep going

Everyone: We Need to Talk

On picking apart myths and misconceptions.
On recognising the extent of sexual violence
and gender-based violence in our societies.
On believing things can change.

We Need To Talk
about myths and narratives

It is easy to talk about sexual violence as something done by faceless male monsters hiding behind bushes at night. Something done to tragically helpless young (white, cis, straight) women too careless to prevent it, too drunk to defend themselves. It is easy to talk about sexual violence as something uncomplicated by ethnicity, class, age, gender, sexuality, ability. Something easily separated from love or family or trust or childhood.

It is easy to talk about sexual violence in this way.
But it is dangerously, murderously simplistic.
And it. Does. Not. Help.

this is not poetry

strip away your
'poetry' goggles
remove your rose-tinted sight
these lines will not smell of flowers
will not speak of butterflies
will not compare thee
to fucking anything
except what you are

I do not write because it is pretty
beauty does not interest me
I write because I fear I would die if I stopped
because silence is killing us
has already killed so many
three last week
three this week
three next week

if you are searching for stories of love and loss
if you want the kind of suffering you can romanticise
if you are looking for me to be tragically beautiful
helpless but lit from all the right angles
go look somewhere else
this book is not for you
my story is not for you
it is mine

my story is not the stock photo
of the white woman cowering
beneath the raised anonymous male hand
my story is not the newspaper pictures
of blurry young women
tilted in on themselves
holding their knees
my story does not exist for your consumption
is not here for you to sell simplistic narratives
of monsters
and victims
in need of saving

if you are looking for every story you have already heard
about rape and abuse
go read a newspaper
and go fuck yourself

myths about rape

if even half the things you have been told about rape
were true
we would live in a very different world

if what you wear
could prevent rape
if you speaking to your friend as they walk home
could prevent rape
if you telling your daughter not to stay out late
could prevent rape
we would live in a very different world

but none of these things prevent rape
they are only the desperate scramblings for sense-making
the clinging to the illusion of control
the terrified hope
that it won't be us
who are raped
tonight

but I promise you
it will be someone
else

like a daily game of russian roulette
we never chose to play
but were born into

only the bullets don't go off
when we press the trigger

because we are not at greatest risk
when we are walking home at night
or when we are drinking
or when we are wearing skirts
or when we are flirting

the bullets go off when and where we should feel safest

nowhere are we as likely to be raped
as in our own beds
no one is as likely to rape us
as someone we trust

as someone we love

if individual choices could prevent rape
this might be a different story
but rape is not a question of risk or choice or morality
it is a question of society
our societies
which rape
has always been part of

pretending this is about individual victims
and not the faults of our entire systems
is failing to understand
why violence happens
violence does not happen because of victims' actions
or inactions
violence is the actions
of perpetrators
it is the result of millions of similar actions
made into silent norm
made systematic
made legitimate
made culture
made normal
over
millennia

the roles we are cast

the roles we are cast
do not fit us
we are not all broken
not all victim
we do not all forgive our rapists
or ever want to

the narrative we are forced into
does not fit us
we do not all want
to hide
to forget
to get over it

some of us
want justice
some of us want change
some of us would rather take revenge
in whatever form we can get

it is not pretty
it shouldn't have to be
we are not all beautifully sad
attractively frail
here for you to save

some of us
are ugly-crying
fury-campaigning
tired of this bullshit
and want our pound of flesh

it is not your right
to judge us
you do not get to decide
what the
'appropriate'
response to rape is

you do not get to feed us our lines
paint our faces
tear-filled but carrying on
airbrush our eyes hopeful

twist our bodies
into poses
of sorrow or despair

we are all of these
none of these
more

you do not get to continue
writing stories where we are saved
by religion
by the police
by having babies

by a good man
by a good cry
by a good haircut and a glass of wine

some of us
would rather save ourselves
leave our caves of isolation
riding the dragon
and slay the knight in shining armour
on our way out

the roles we are cast
we did not choose ourselves
you did
or history did
or tradition did
and nothing's changed
you want our stories
to entertain you
to please you
to make you comfortable
only that's not what we came here to do

we came to make some noise
to hijack narratives written
about
but never
for us

we came to reclaim our stories
to start this conversation on our own terms
we came
to fuck shit up

we are here
to survive
you do not get to decide
how we should do it

age of violence

abuse doesn't start in college
or when you're old enough to drink

abuse doesn't end in the retirement home
or when you're too old to drive

gender-based violence
doesn't have an age bracket
sexual violence isn't sexy

if you don't hear
about rape victims over eighty-five
or childhood abuse
it is not because it doesn't happen

it's because we've made those stories
even harder
for the victims
to tell

not your story

dear journalists
dear fiction writers
dear TV producers
let's get one thing straight

we are
not your sexual tropes
not the punchbag punchline
of your rape jokes
not your weak virgin victims
versus
monstrous not-all-men
we are not your us and them
not your but then again

we are
not your blushing brides
not your helpless heroines
not your *suit yourselves*
not your *what did you expect going dressed like that*
not your
you have no one
but yourself
to blame

we are
not your hero makers
not your honour to defend
not your male protagonist's motivation for revenge
not your mechanism of punishment
not your plot twist
not your narrative that persistently dismissing all our *nos*
was how we fell
and we are not
your story
to tell

we are
not your newspaper headlines
about the athletic track records
of our rapists
not your *poor perpetrators'*
'shattered careers'

not your Oscar winners' and presidents'
'bad ideas'
not your *but the rapist seems so nice*
not your victim blame and disbelief
not your demands that our rape kits
be publically published online
not your verdict by popular trial
of the victim

we are not your truth to define

we are
not your simplistic tragic backstory
not your weak victims
or strong survivors
not your binary code
not your either/or
not your sexual fantasy to misspell
and not your story to tell

we are
not your romanticised rape in every TV series
not your tingling titillation
not your normalisation
of sexual violence *as entertainment*
not your tired old excuse of
'but every female character getting raped is
historically accurate'
we are not your Stockholm Syndrome
Beauty and the Beast Belle
and we are not your story to tell

so who are we?
we are all the lived experiences of rape
you never hear
over the noise of
all
this
fiction

we are
one in two trans and non-binary folk
we are

one in three women
we are
one in five men
we are
one in five children

we are
the public secret we have learned to live with
and never tell

and we are
not your fucking story
to sell

We Need To Talk about sexual violence and gender-based violence

A terrifying number of people have experienced sexual violence in their lifetime. A horrifying, heartbreaking number of people have been assaulted or abused. And each experience is different. Each trauma and each road to recovery is different.

I cannot represent all these stories. What I can do is scrape the surface of the iceberg that is sexual violence in our societies. What I can do is point under the water's surface and say
LOOK
and say
LISTEN
and say
we need to take this seriously
we need to talk about this properly
we need to change this
NOW

And that is what I am doing in this book.

definitions

let's get our facts straight

rape
is not someone
losing control
of themselves

it is someone
choosing
to use violence
to control
someone else

public secret

gender-based violence
is a public secret
it means we all know it happens
but would rather pretend we don't

sexual violence
is a public secret
we all know someone who has been raped
but none of us want to admit
to knowing a rapist

when an entire host of crimes
affecting the majority of the population
on a daily basis
become public secrets
(become?
haven't they always been?
this might be the longest passed down public secret
in human history)

when something this gigantic
is a public secret
we are all complicit
in the silencing of victims

if we will not admit
to these crimes being everyday
and ordinary
to abuse being committed by 'nice guys'
to rape being the action of 'family men'
to women and parents and carers also being abusers

if we will not admit to these things
we make it impossible
for victims
to *admit* to what has happened to them
to *speak* about what has happened to them
to *report* what has happened to them
and to be believed

because public secrets are always rather not spoken of
always make people uncomfortable
when brought to the light

because
'but he's such a good guy,
I can't believe he would do that'
and
'it's just a little domestic,
don't make a big thing of it'
are how we silence victims

because the only way through
is to speak

we need to talk

this body is a home

this body
is a home
I searched for one
so long
inside others
searched for a place
to be at bay
in cities and lovers
families and jobs

finally
I found it
in the pit of myself
at the core of me
in my body

this body
is safety
I had that
stolen and toyed with
broken and bruised
by abuse
and now
I am reclaiming it all
repurposing every cell
for my defences
my comfort
my self

this body
is a safe zone
in the war
on bodies like and unlike mine
it is a haven
a panic room
a bomb cellar
a ceasefire
a peace of sorts

this body
is a weapon
against the dehumanisation
of our bodies

the attempt at rendering
the traumas inflicted
on us
in us
every day
entirely incidental

calling them sexual assault
calling them homophobic or transphobic hate crime
calling them xenophobic attacks
as if our bodies, our homes
were attacked
by no one in particular
for no particular reason

as if it were lightning that struck us
as if it were the natural order of things
as if it were an unavoidable natural disaster

as if no one were responsible
as if no one were to blame
as if there were nothing that could be done
to prevent this

these bodies
are homes
our homes

ain't no one
taking that away from us
again

coral reef

some days
I feel I am standing
on a coral reef
of dead women
layering one upon the other

three killed by their partners
last week alone
three the week before
and the week before
and the week before

below them
twelve last month
one hundred and forty-four last year
how many last decade
last century
?

three upon three upon three
the reef has been building
underneath the surface
for millennia

we do not talk about the violence
that happens behind closed doors
we do not talk about the violence
that leaves no visible bruises
we do not talk about
what happens beneath marital sheets
in couples' flats
under the roofs of
'perfectly ordinary'
families

we do not talk
and for years
the silence has been bubbling away
drowning us

I feel as if I am standing
on a coral reef
of dead women

so many generations
of silences lie buried here
so many unspoken truths

what stories would they have told
if we had let them?
what stories would they have told
had we not silenced them
with
'a little domestic is nothing to worry about'
and 'everyone has a rough patch'
and 'that's best kept quiet'
?

some days
I feel I am standing
on a coral reef
of dead women
layered through all of human history

but here
at the end of this long line of suffering
here
at the top of this funeral pyre
here
I am

standing

and after all these deaths
all these unreported and unspoken-of
lives
here I am
standing

and finally
maybe
finally
we are close enough to breaking the surface
that our voices will be heard

We Need To Talk about rape culture and structural sexual violence

Sexual violence is done to people of all genders, all ethnicities, all religions, classes, abilities and ages. But it is not done in equal measure. Those most vulnerable and most oppressed – those whose lives and bodies exist in the intersection of several systems of oppression – are most likely to be targeted by sexual violence and gender-based violence. Disabled women are twice as likely as other women to experience sexual abuse. Trans women and trans femmes of colour face a higher risk of murder than any other group of people. Gender-based violence is not incidental.

The people who are most oppressed are most often targeted by sexual violence – but these groups of people are also least likely to get access to support services, to protection, to legal justice.

Oppression, inequality and structural violence against victims often continues in support services, police departments and courtrooms. When this happens, we have failed to address the root problems of gender-based violence. And we have failed the victims.

Understanding the structural nature of violence is the only way we can begin to change it. So make an effort to understand.

my trauma is political

my trauma isn't private
is not about me
not really
it is about our failure
to stop this happening
again and again
to so many millions
so many more than me

sometimes when you reach deep inside yourself
it helps to connect your experience to the statistics
your life to the big picture

because the view of your pillow as he –
because the particular repeated pain as he continued to –
because that is not what this story is about

my rapist does not exist in a vacuum
my rape is not a story about me
not really
it is a story about a time we live in
a system we live under
a structure of violence
that has been normalised

my trauma is political

rape as risk

neoliberalism
frames rape as risk
in other words
rape is not seen as a societal issue with structural causes
but a problem individuals have the responsibility to negotiate
prevent and protect themselves from

the question does not become
'how do we make sure people do not rape?'
or even
'how do we make sure people do not get raped?'
but rather
'how do I make sure I am not the one who is raped
since rape will inevitably happen?'

this might seem like a small difference
but it's not

the difference is that the responsibility
for ending sexual violence
is not placed on the collective
the society
the culture
the state
but on the individual

the difference is that
the global structural epidemic of sexual violence
is cast as a series of problems
caused by individual victims' choices
and solved by potential victims making different choices

the difference is that
sexual violence does not become a question
of programmes to change attitudes
prevent crime
and prosecute criminals
but a question of the individual's risk-taking
(and moral) behaviour
what not to wear
where not to walk
what not to say
drink

do
be
in order to not put yourself
at 'risk'
of rape

nowhere is this clearer
than in neoliberalism's most striking form of individualism
private health insurance

increasingly
in countries with high sexual violence
and neoliberal ideologies of public responsibility
the 'risk' of rape is calculated into the cost of health care
women's private health insurance
is more expensive in India and South Africa
because it includes a 'rape premium'
take that in for a moment

rape
is so statistically likely to happen to women in these countries
that they are asked to cover the cost
of physical and psychological rehabilitation
from rape
ahead of time

not only
are we held personally responsible
for being raped
we also have to pay in advance
for the likelihood of it happening

if that is not blaming the victim
if that is not absolving the perpetrator
if that is not placing the cost of violence on the individual
the responsibility of ending violence on the oppressed

if that is not the pinnacle of rape culture
I don't know what is

dew drops

1.
a rape survivor
is told by her university
not to attend classes
as she brings bad reputation to the school
her rapist can keep studying

2.
five men who have raped a disabled classmate
are freed on all charges
because it cannot be proven
whether *all* or *some* of them
committed the rape

3.
a boy
is told it can't have been rape
because boys
always want sex
or at least they *should*

4.
a woman
is killed by her partner
while attempting to leave abuse
the police have been called to her house
three times before and done nothing

I cannot be the only person
exhausted from collecting these stories
tired of the lack of happy endings
the lack of change
the lack of hope
the lack of
anything
new

they are heavy
these dew drops of suffering we are collecting
each mo(u)rning
each day

in making the personal political
in weaving narrative
uncovering structure
from all these 'one-offs'
all these instances of violence
all these symptoms of the underlying disease

it is heavy
to be a carrier of stories like this
it is heavy

but as much as we try to look away
that is not an option
and so we carry them

the people and their stories
we carry them

thin leaves in morning sunlight
only just beginning to find the sun ourselves
we carry them
all these dew drops
all these stories
of what happened
during this night

as it happened the night before
and will happen again tonight

when the light returns
we take inventory of the suffering

how many rapes since last night?
how many hate crimes?
how many murders?

we collect these stories
carry them for those who did not survive
carry them for those not yet able
to hold the weight of their own memories

we carry them
to the best of our abilities

we carry them
as we wished others
had carried us

only dew drops
each and every one
but together
amounting
to an ocean

we are arming perpetrators

if you have ever wondered
why so many victims of rape and abuse
do not report what has happened to them
do not speak about what has happened to them
all you have to do
is consider how victims of sexual violence are treated

it is shockingly rare
that a perpetrator is punished
in even the most basic legal way
but in every case
in all cases
the victim is punished

social punishment
emotional and psychological punishment
punishment through rumour-spreading
punishment through retraumatisation
punishment through disbelief and doubt

when rape occurs at a school
most often it is the victim
that is forced to drop out
that is forced to move
that is forced to change their whole life

most rapists
experience no amount
of shame or guilt campaigns
no amount of blame or retaliation
even comparable to what *every* victim experiences

this process
of blaming the victim for the crime
of punishing the victim for the crime
is far from limited to schools

when people say
'well, what did they think, going dressed like that?'
when people say
'they should have known better than to drink with those boys'
when people say
'none of this would have happened if the victim had just…'

what they are really saying
is the victim is to blame
for the crime committed against them

and somehow
the perpetrator goes free
not just legally
but socially
somehow the perpetrator is not responsible
for the crime
they have committed
somehow
the victim is

HOW?

do you know
of any other crime
where we treat victims like this?
because I don't

by questioning victims' stories
by doubting victims
by speaking about victims in hushed tones
as they pass down corridors
as they report their abuse
as they are written about in gossip magazines

by speaking *about* victims
instead of speaking *to* them
instead of listening to them
instead of believing them

by punishing victims for what has been done to them
we are arming perpetrators

we are arming perpetrators in their threats
that if the victim speaks
no one will believe them

we are arming perpetrators in their threats
to release revenge porn
to send photos or videos

of the victim's naked body
to the victim's parents
or classmates
or football coaches
or partner

we are arming perpetrators
in continuing their abuse

and when
teenage girls
who have been targeted by assault
and online grooming
are so afraid of what will happen to them
if they tell
of how we will judge them
of how we will blame them
of how we will punish them
that they attempt suicide

then their blood is on our hands
because we have been arming perpetrators

because our treatment of victims
has armed predators
and left victims
defenceless
and it needs
to stop

We Need To Talk about criminal (in)justice, police and politics

Sexual violence and gender-based violence are not natural phenomena, not things that 'just happen' and for no reason.

Structural sexual violence is the result of structural inequalities – and a way to maintain those inequalities. Sexual violence is a tool to maintain systems of power and hierarchy. Sexual violence is a recognised weapon of war.

And it is deeply intertwined with systems of criminal (in)justice, with police brutality, and with politics of fear.

The only way to fight it is political.

witch trials

*(no court practices are as intrusive, as inconclusive
and as victim-focused as rape trials
nowhere else is the victim interrogated so much
and the perpetrator interrogated so little)*

*a witch trial
of rape victims*

float
and be damned
for lying
for insufficient evidence
for not getting your rape kit
to the police
before the rape itself had finished
for the police losing the evidence

burn
at the stake of gossip-mongers
at the disbelief of those you trusted

drown
and be innocent
of your own rape

but guilty
somehow
of bringing it on yourself

fear is a physical creature

he hides between my ribs
slithers up my spine
aches in my stomach
living with fear is being always alone
and never alone

living in times of fear
of politics of fear
being warned again and again
about the future that might be
the future that might make all other futures

impossible

living in times of fear
is being always isolated
is trust always being a calculated risk
is risk always being managed
never undone

fear is a physical creature
we cannot fight it with rationality
arguments does not make it go away
it is there
always

in bed with us
in our dreams
as we eat our food
dress our bodies
walk out into a world
that frightens us

people say that fear comes of experience
and many of us have lived reasons to fear
many of us
live with online violence
as part of our daily lives
many of us live with fear of attack and assault
fear of police brutality and hate crime
as part of our bodies
many of us live with fear
as a result of who we are

grinding against the sharp edges
of the status quo

but in times of politics of fear
even the privileged
even the powerful
even the normative
live with fear clinging to their backs

in times of violent nationalism
and threats of violence breaking out

all of us sleep next to fear at night
because fear is a physical creature
we do not choose it
it enters our lives and stays there
until a time when we feel safe again
some of us never do

it is in what we do to build that safety
that we decide how to deal with the creature that is fear
do we deal by arming ourselves
by distrusting everybody
by doubting all intentions?

or do we decide to trust
this unimaginable incalculable leap of faith?
do we decide to build something with others
that is bigger than our fear
bigger than our safety
bigger than ourselves?

do we undo fear's power over us
unclench fear's claws
or do we try to wrap our claws around others?

those are the questions fear asks us
that is where all fear leads

and I for one
choose trust
choose change
choose togetherness

the police

the police
arrive at Women's Aid
take my testimony
look me up and down
ask
if you were really abused
why didn't you just leave?

the police
leave me a number to call
for victim support
when I call the number
they tell me they have no support services
for abuse survivors
would I consider a nunnery?

the police tell me
don't speak to anyone
don't trust anyone
but don't be afraid
also
your rapist might try to sue
for defamation
so don't speak
stay quiet

the police tell me
don't call us
we'll call you
the police do not call
for five months

in the meantime
I cry in bathrooms
have panic attacks on buses
struggle to get out of bed
in the meantime
I develop PTSD

the police call
after five months
to tell me they are closing the investigation
they believe I was raped

but can't prove it
my rapist is threatening to sue me
the police tell me
the witnesses are threatening to sue me
the police tell me
so don't speak

the police tell me
don't speak
don't provoke your rapist
the police are already at capacity
under-resourced, you see
so don't put another case on our table
so don't speak

afterwards
after they wait for more victims to come forward
there have been more victims, they're sure
they speak on social media
but won't talk to the police
the police
can't understand why

afterwards
after my case has been closed
the local police department
wins an award for having a
'cutting edge'
domestic violence support unit

the police officer
who told me not to speak
accepts the award

dangerous people

the man who robbed me
did not announce himself as robber
instead he knocked on my door
and kindly asked to be let in
knew the name of the landlord
said he was there to fix the roof
instead he came into my life
a relief

'we've been expecting you,' I said
as I opened the door and let my robber in

he needed to get an adapter, he said
for one of his tools, he said
and he circled the rooms, looking for one
it bothered me
but not enough to ask him to stop
he needed one more tool, he said
he'd just get it from his car, he said
he'd just pop out and get it, he said
and he left through the front door

as he closed the door behind him
he left me with final words
'don't want to be letting any robbers in
now do we?'

as the door clicked into place
I felt a sigh of relief
by the time I realised how much
had been stolen he was far gone

the moral of the story is
the most dangerous people
always claim
they want to protect you
from *dangerous* people

the man who raped me
did not announce himself rapist

instead he came into my life
quoting feminism
fundraising for rape crisis centres

asking to walk me home at night
to keep me safe, he said
from people who wanted to harm me, he said
there were people who wanted to harm me, he said
but not him

years down the line
when rape had become part of my daily life
still living alongside this man of excuses
he still said this
he wanted to protect me
from people who wanted to harm me
but he used different words now
practised different excuses

'I love you and I would never harm you,' he said
he used this as a mantra
every day
as if his words could undo his deeds
remake the world in his image
erase the harm he'd done to me
the night before
and the night before
and the night before

the moral of the story is
the people who say they are strong enough
to protect you
also know they are strong enough
to harm you

the moral of the story is
the most dangerous people
always say they want to protect you
from *someone else*

the politicians that will oppress us
will not announce themselves oppressors
instead they will name themselves

our protectors
our saviours

instead they will promise

to make us
great again
instead they will point to distant threats
and promise to protect us
with walls and deportations
to keep us safe
from 'swarms' and 'invasions'

instead they will mutter words like
terror
as if they belonged to someone else
as if they could remake the world
in their image

as if wars fought for oil were not terror
as if children killed by drones were not terror
as if racism and Islamophobia were not violence
as if austerity and cuts did not leave real people bleeding

oppressors have never come into power
announcing themselves oppressors
they come into power claiming to be
champions of the people
claiming to speak for the common man
they come into power promising to
protect you from *dangerous* people
they come into power promising they will
make you great again
pure again
true again

you are smart enough to know better than that
to see through the rhetoric
to not repeat the same mistake
repeated throughout human history

the moral of the story is
the people who say they want to protect you

from dangerous people
are the most dangerous people

the moral of the story is
in order to convince you

that they can save you
they need to first convince you
that you need saving

so I will say it once
in the hope to never have to say it again

we do not need saving

Victims and Survivors: We Need to Talk

On coping and creating, support and siblinghood.
On learning that you are believed, that you are not alone and that it really, truly wasn't your fault.
On ending rape culture, and the fight still ahead of us.

Victims And Survivors: We Need To Talk about surviving

Each experience of violence is different. And no road to recovery is the same. Whatever you need to do to keep safe, to keep going and to cope, do that. Here are some words to help you on the way. Keep what is helpful to you, and leave the rest.

To you, who have suffered sexual assault or abuse.
However you are doing at the moment.
However recent or distant violence feels.
Wherever you are in your recovery and sense-making.

To you, I want to say this:
You are not at fault. You are not on trial. And you are not alone.

I believe you.

And I promise: things are going to be OK. Really, they are.

I wish someone had told me

you are enough
just as you are
I promise you
you are enough

it won't always be this hard
I promise you
it won't always be this hard

just surviving requires tremendous strength
and you are that strong
I promise you

I believe in you
I promise you
I believe in you

you will find a way to get through this
even if you don't know how
yet
I promise
you will find a way

it all begins
when you forgive yourself
for this happening to you
trust yourself
that you will get through
love yourself
again
I promise you
it is OK if you're not there yet

you are not alone
I promise you
you are not alone

this is what I wish someone had told me
and now
that I know it to be true
I am telling you

you are not alone
I believe you
you will get through this

unbreakable

I don't want to be broken
don't want to be traumatised
don't want to be victim
but if I am

to stop lying to myself
if I am
to stop denying what has
happened
to me
if I am
to admit to this

let me not be broken
alone
let me be fractured along the same lines
as all who've suffered rape and abuse
let the shards of our fractures
fit into each other
origami structures
folding into one another

if I am
to be broken
let us together form a whole
let there
at least
be solidarity
in this trauma

let me not be left to battle it alone
if I am to admit
to victim
let there be a glimpse
of future
in which we will stand together
as survivors
strong and proud

and when fitted
arm in arm
shard in shard
let us be
unbreakable

how to suffer

how to suffer
without anyone noticing:

lie
to keep your abuser safe

lie
about how much they're harming you

lie
every time someone asks you
if you are OK

lie to your friends
to your family
to your co-workers
to your counsellor

most of all
lie to yourself

and then stop

how to survive

keep moving forwards
keep checking in on yourself
keep talking to those you trust

find a small goal
like getting out of bed
or eating a proper meal
or going for a walk
or rereading your favourite book
or watching your favourite TV series
work towards that goal
and then another
and then another

take small steps
understand that they are giant

imagine what safety feels like
looks like
sounds like
smells like
tastes like
and then bring yourself there
in your mind
when things get too hard
breathe
breathe
breathe

treat yourself
the way you would
a small child
or a cuddly animal
understand that you are
a hurt creature
requiring love
and care
and nurturing

watch yourself grow
into something stronger
something mightier
something with skin thick enough

it might be mistaken for armour
unbreakable enough
that you can feel safe
within yourself

become
a dragon
a hero
a protagonist of your own story
spread your wings
raise your sword
tell your truth

repeat when necessary
survive

Victims And Survivors: We Need To Talk about fighting

I know telling the truth can be unbearably hard. I know that admitting to yourself – much less admitting to someone else – what has been done to you can be unthinkable.

I know there's a fight that starts the second violence begins. One that does not end when violence is finished.

I know that the path to recovery, to healing, to trust, to hope, to change, can be long and winding and fucking infuriating.

I don't know what things are like for you right now. But I know this: hold on. For another breath, another word, another night's sleep. Hold on and things will get a little easier, and then a lot easier, and then so great you can't even imagine it right now.

Just hold on.

dear future self having a panic attack

remember your breath
remember you can always find it
in the pit of your stomach
in the core of yourself

remember it will always bring you back
to the land of the living
to the present moment
it will take you away
from what you cannot bear
to remember right now
if only you wait
for the next inhale
and the next
and the next

dear future self
having a panic attack
remember all the living you've done
after violence

look forward to all the living
you have yet to do

you have so much more to experience
to accomplish
to become

remember all of that
is still ahead of you
just take another step
and another
another breath
and another

you are getting there
I promise

dear future self
having a panic attack
remember you are free from violence now
you left it
you walked out

and it will not catch up with you again
you have come too far for that
have worked too hard
don't let the shadow of their voice
still nestling in your head
convince you otherwise

dear future self
having a panic attack
remember the people you love
and who love you
remember the people who care for you
and who you care for

finally
remember yourself
you can get through this
you have already survived
so much worse

all this is
is aftershocks
all this is
is a reminder
that the worst is over

and you have
so much better
to look forward to

I imagine safety

I try to imagine
somewhere safe
for some reason
the place that comes to mind
is a spaceship
with a broken comm
outside a dead solar system

I imagine
me
and food
and tea
and a cat for company

just me and space
me and time
me and the stars
and safety

I imagine
a chosen solitude
a place where no one could reach me
and all the problems
that used to feel
unmanageable
are suddenly
miniscule
from this
galactically
far away

I imagine safety
and harm
can't reach me
anymore

surface

sometimes
I feel my life
is a series of excavations

as if I am only ever
searching my past
looking to save
something
some shred of hope
from these underwater ruins
to bring to the surface with me

because yes
life grows down here
seaweeds and corals
are springing up
in the cracks of dead places
but this new life
is only ever accidental
only ever in spite of the ruins
the crisis
the way things fall apart

life never seems to exist
without a relationship to what was before
the reason the ship sank
the whys of the ocean rising

and I am tired
of excavating
tired of searching the past
for answers
the pressure of being
so far under water
for so long
is getting to me

sometimes
I just want to look up
see the light filter through the water
and break the surface

leave behind

what hides beneath the water
and believe instead
that our best
and most revolutionary days

are still ahead of us

floating

I am out of words
this does not happen often
words are what I do
who I am
what I live by and on and for

but here I am
out of words
speechless

I have searched for words
clung to them like
lifeboats
words like
psychological abuse
kept me afloat
shackled my terror
my fear and confusion
onto something tangible
words like
post-traumatic stress disorder
were the storm clearing
and the shore
on the horizon

I have clung to words
to keep from drowning
gathered them around me like life vests
like relief from this endless treading of water

and now I find
I am out of words
paralysed
and unable to swim
but somehow
I am still floating
still hanging on
to what
– hope?

the counsellor says
if you can't find the words right now
if you don't know what to do

or what's next
maybe we can just sit with that
for now
let it be what it is
?

I don't see what other options I have
so we sit there
quietly
floating
holding on to something
like hope

things I know for sure (a meditation for survivors)

repeat after me:

I am loved
I am always loved
because I love myself

I am cared for
I am always cared for
because I will care for myself

I am safe
I will make sure I am safe
because now I know
because now I know for certain
that if I need to
I can break out of any cage
escape any danger
if I need to
I can make myself mighty and invisible at once
and I can get myself into safety

I am not alone
so many people have walked this path before me
so many have been distrusted and doubted
so many have been retraumatised and disbelieved
so many have gone through just what I have gone through
in their own ways

I will not be doubted
I will not be disbelieved
for every person I have to cut contact with
every situation I have to leave
there stands a person before me
to guide me through it
there stands a person after me
who I will help get through

I am not my rape
I am not my abuse
I am not my trauma

these are a fraction of the experiences of my life

I will sew them into the patchwork of my story
with gold thread
with honesty and care
and I will wear them proudly

knowing always
knowing completely
that
this
too
shall
pass

Victims And Survivors: We Need To Talk about living again

There is an 'after' that starts at some point after violence, and some distance into processing and recovering. It does not mean violence has stopped affecting you. But it does mean that there is distance between yourself and violence. At least in some ways.

At least some days. It may be that you are still dealing with the aftereffects of violence: with legal processes or large life changes. It may be that you are battling with physical or mental ill-health. With PTSD or anxiety disorder or depression. It may be that getting back to 'normal' feels everything but.

Perhaps it feels like you are ready to start living again. In that case, you will not be alone in what comes next.

surprised

when I wake up
and feel good
I am surprised
still
unused to the sensation
acutely aware
of how I can't take it for granted
afraid it could leave
at any time

when I wake up
and feel safe
I am surprised
still
there is a discomfort
to slipping so easily into your own skin
the frictionlessness of it
when for years
you were always ready
to jump out of it

there's a normalcy after abuse
that does not come
there is a gratefulness
a surprise
a newness
that prods at you when you wake

they say
when someone you love dies
the first few minutes each morning are the hardest
that moment when you go from thinking they are alive
to remembering they're not

with abuse (with me)
it's the opposite
the first moments between sleep and wakefulness
you are still scared
still tense
still fight-or-flight-or-freeze
and then
you remember
you left

and it's like the clouds parting
the sunlight streaming in

each morning
a reminder
to say thank you
to yourself
thank you
for taking such good care of yourself
thank you, self
for leaving
and for learning
slowly
to live again

provincialising violence

once violence
is introduced
into your life
it does not leave

but with time
and with backbreaking work
it becomes less central
it stops residing at the core of you
occupying you
keeping your life under siege

admitting that violence has been done to you
sends it out from the central squares of your heart
and down dark alleyways

talking about it
forces it out on country roads
towards peripheral provinces of who you are

processing it
pushes it towards the edges of you
towards the middle of nowhere
and then past it
to the outskirts
to the folds in the map
to the edges of your world

you do not finish
with violence
but your provincialise it
you render it non-central, non-essential

with time
and with heartbreaking work
the burden of carrying violence
becomes lighter to bear
you carry each scrap of it
towards the edges of your map
and return lighter

with time
you stop walking the dusty roads

out to it
again and again
you memorialise it
and leave it to become ruins
something ancient and near-forgotten

with time
you plant seeds in the ground
allow weeds to grow
and something fruitful
something beautiful
to cover the once well-worn tracks
to those memories

you do not stop being affected by violence
but you provincialise it
and rebuild yourself
stronger

technicolor

there are days
I am beyond grateful
and into joy
days I beam with warmth
glow from within
remember with pride
all the adventures
that only months ago
I never dreamed
I would live
moments
I did not actually believe
I would be alive to experience

I pay attention to things now
things I never used to
like the seasons changing
I take all the time I want
in my favourite bookshops now
stay awake with the calm
of that final cup of tea now
and every time I see a low-hanging leaf
from a tree
I jump up to touch it
with a childish joy
I never thought I'd have again

some days
leaving violence
feels like getting your life back
in technicolor

I'll save you a seat

there are days
I go out walking
just to feel the sun on my face
just to feel the air in my lungs
just to laugh with the joy
of being alive

and here I sit
on a park bench
crying with gratefulness
I am alive
I am alive
I am alive

there were times
I wasn't sure
I would be
when it was impossible to imagine
anything other than
breath upon breath upon breath
one at a time
and even that
was damn near impossible

but there is a time
after
I promise
there is a time after violence
really
there is
and it is beautiful
I promise you
you will get there too
just hold on
for another breath
and another

there will be a time
when you go walking
just to laugh out loud
with the joy of being alive
it might not seem like it
but I promise
it's true

there will be a time after violence
I promise you
just hold on
hold on
and one day
perhaps very soon
one day
you'll find yourself
walking
and smiling at the sun
on your face

and you'll find me
there in the park
sitting on a bench
looking at the future
with hope

I promise

I'll save you a seat

Victims And Survivors: We Need To Talk about the fight still ahead of us

This is the heavy truth I have realised: recovery, for me, is not enough.

When life begins again, so does the realisation that this happens to so many people. That I don't want them to have to go through what I have gone through. That we need to team up, and wise up, and start to change things.

Perhaps this is how you feel too. That our traumas are reminders of the political work ahead of us – in building community and support and solidarity. For and with and alongside other survivors. That the fight ahead lies in changing attitudes, in changing laws, and, ultimately, in changing the world.

the circle

to anyone in doubt
anyone in fear
anyone worried
about how to talk about what has happened to them
– in short, to you –
I want to say

do not listen
to the echoes of the status quo
to the voices wishing to silence you
they are loud
but so few

and there are
so many of us
standing here
strongly
surely

I promise you

we have been placing our feet in a circle
facing outwards
protecting people just like you
for months and years
for decades and centuries
for as long as there has been sexual violence
meaning
for as long as any history we know of
for all that time
we have been building our defences

and when you are ready
when you feel strong enough
when you have grieved and raged
and bashed your heart against rock bottom

when you are ready to get back up

come join us
there is a spot here
waiting for you
in the circle

just come stand with us

a revolution of sorts

I am tired
of people talking about happiness
as a choice
devoid of context

I am tired
of hearing happiness mentioned
in the same breath
as beetroot juice
and self-employment

we know
we know from the research
the qualitative and the quantitative
the lifelong and the at-a-glance
that mental health is impacted by structures

that sexism and racism
that homophobia and transphobia
that ableism and ageism and inequality
have measurable effects on mental health
that gender-based violence results in PTSD
that colonialism has been inherited as trauma
that poverty and war
are not things you brush off
as you reach for your bootstraps

we know
that happiness is not a choice
and mental health is not devoid of context
we cannot blame ourselves
for living in a world that wears on us
gets inside our clothes
sticks to thoughts and emotions

we are not to blame for our suffering
we are not to blame for our struggling
we are not to blame for the world we were born into

but now that we are here
now that we are here

maybe there is space

for emancipation
maybe there is space
for empowerment
maybe there is space
for us to take our happiness as our own

to decide that our refusal
to buckle under
is hope
that our wellbeing
is resistance
that our resilience

is a revolution of sorts

the end of the tunnel

I want to talk to you
because I think you might be lonely
because I get lonely too

I want to talk to you
because I've been there
because hopelessness is suffocating
because silence is death
because enough has to be enough

I want to talk to you
because there's a
TOGETHER
for us to meet in
because this is more than
instance upon instance
because this is more than
in this case
because there is no such thing
as unconnected violence

I want to talk to you
because the distance between us
is impenetrable darkness
and it can start to close in on me
and then
and there
I need a path forward
a way past and on
and I think you're it

I think we can build this path
together
like a bridge
I think we can stand our ground
together
like a dam
I think we can end
the constant flow of violence

I really do

I think we can help those

who come after us
I think we can learn from those
who came before us
I think we can be the in-between
where all our stories meet

I think there's a light
at the end of the tunnel
and it's where our fingertips meet
and it's where our arms link
and it's where our voices join

what do we do?

what do we do
when the violence is over?
when it feels like it will never really end?

what do we do
when we're no longer in danger
but never really feel safe?

what do we do with the rest of our lives?
the rest of our day?
with those mornings when everything already feels lost?

what do we do with the violence?

we speak
we speak because we have to
because the alternative is suffocation
is going back under the surface again
is giving in to our abusers' voices
in the backs of our heads
is letting violence win

we listen
we listen for the other voices
the ones that remind us we are not alone in this
that we will never be alone in this again
that there are those who've walked our paths
those who can help illuminate the next step
or just make sure we are not alone
as we figure out our own journeys

we change
more than ourselves
and more than adaptation
more than the bad days
sometimes so unbearable
all you can do is hold on
and wait it out
more than the good days
sometimes so glorious
so sunshine-filled
we doubt whether the bad days
ever truly happened

more than ourselves
we change together
we build support
communities
movements

more than ourselves
we change the culture that put us here
the systems that enabled and enforced this

more than ourselves
we change the world

Friends and Family: We Need to Talk

On the things every survivor needs to hear you say.
On understanding what your loved one is going through.
On how to respond, how to support
and your job from now on.

Friends And Family: We Need To Talk about understanding

When someone close to you has been abused or assaulted (and, statistically speaking, several people you know have been), you need to think about how to be there for them. Even if you are not aware of someone in your immediate surroundings who has been the victim of sexual violence, the terrifying odds are that someone close to you will be, and soon.

This is a guide for learning to understand, to listen to and support your loved one on their terms. Because the alternative is a whole host of people in your life silently deciding they can't trust you.

This is a first step towards being the support they need.
I implore you to take it.

things I did to cope

walk
run
lie perfectly still

talk to no one
talk to everyone
talk to a counsellor

exercise
eat
sleep
repeat

speak honestly
with myself

write
write
write

constantly eat carrot sticks
(to give my hands something to do)

listen to audio books around the clock
(to not have to hear my own thoughts)

go to meditation classes
yoga classes
forests
(to get a break from the panic)

obsessively watch Disney films
(to imagine I could have a happy ending)

whatever helped me
feel better
feel OK
feel like myself

and finally
write
this
book

trust

how do you tell people you love
that you no longer trust them?

that the rules of your trust have been rewritten
and you no longer know them by heart
that your trust has been bruised and broken
too many times

and now
your trust is a shy thing
it needs coaxing
it needs reassurances
and if there is so much as one misstep
one raised voice
one hand placed where it was not invited
one disbelieving comment
about people like you
people who've gone through what you have gone through
then your trust will refuse to come out entirely
for weeks and months and years
maybe ever

because it doesn't matter what used to be safe
nothing is anymore
instead you are
always on edge
always guilty about how you feel
always searching for exits
to anywhere you meet
anyone you meet
any conversation that you have
instead you are hoping to avoid your way out
of a relationship that causes you
that much anxiety
that much worry
that much fear

even if it is someone you love
a best friend
or a partner
or a parent

loving someone
doesn't change
any of that

the bell (jar)

there are mornings I wake up from nightmares
and I don't remember them
but I remember who was there
he was there again
they were there again
and for a second
I forget I left
for a second
I forget I got out
I got out alive
I am still alive
and for a second
I forget to be thankful for that

the burden gets easier to bear
but not then
not there
not in half-sleep
not at my most vulnerable
when I am not yet sure who else might be in the room
and what they might do to me when I wake

it took me months
to learn to sleep in the same room as another person
I kept a bell
on the handle of my bedroom door
for a year
woke up every time someone walked in the hallway
as my bell moved from their steps

every morning
I went from nightmares to the gym
in less than five minutes
trying to breathe and stretch and sweat
the panic out of me
and most days it worked

but the next night
I placed the bell on the handle
just the same
it was the only way
I could feel safe enough
to sleep

surviving

I can't remember
what it felt like
when trauma
wasn't part of me

people keep telling me
I am brave
for fighting this fight
that I am strong
for taking this issue on

people keep telling me
it must take so much work
just to get from one day to the next

people keep telling me
'I don't know how you do it'

and the truth is
I don't remember
how you don't

psychological abuse

they weaponised
my silences
declared war
on my consent
forced apart
every last piece of what held me
together

and then
when I was already broken
gaslighted my memory
set fire
to my truth

so that in the end
the person it was most difficult
to convince
that what had been done to me
was abuse

the person
it was most difficult
to persuade away from doubt
was myself

and still
I did it

an ordinary life

there is a beauty to the ordinary
to eating your breakfast in peace
to doing your laundry in peace
to cooking your food
to petting your cat
to watering your plants
in peace

when for years
your life was without peace
when for years
violence was your ordinary

there is a joy
to living in a house
you have never been raped in
sleeping in a bed
you have never been raped in
dressing in clothes
your abuser has never forced off you
never even seen

there is a joy
there is a beauty
there is a brilliance and a calm
to a life free from violence

when for years
violence was all you knew

when for years
violence was sewn into your clothes
violence seeped into your mattress
violence shaped and coloured
your every dream
your every thought
your every feeling about yourself and the world

there is a joy to this ordinary life
so don't you dare tell me I'm settling
when only months ago
I couldn't have dared dream
as big as this

an ordinary life
a life free from violence

Friends And Family: We Need To Talk about your role in all of this

I noticed quickly that some people understood how to respond when I told them about my abuse. They knew how to say, 'I am so sorry *that* this happened to you,' and to stay far away from the disbelief and doubt of 'I am sorry *if* that happened to you.'

They knew how to hold my hand. To remind me to keep eating. To check in on me, several times a week. To let me do whatever brought me joy or calm. Even if it was obsessively reading chick lit. Even if it was eating ridiculous amounts of carrot sticks. Even if my coping mechanisms made no sense to them. They were there for me. Without me needing to ask.

But there were other people who did not know how to respond, or made no effort to support me. Some of those people failed so miserably in responding with empathy, or care, or action, that they reinforced my abuse. That they added to my retraumatisation. That I lost all trust in them, and eventually broke all contact.

Understanding your role in someone's recovery is the difference between them being able to trust you and you harming them further. Take that as life-and-deathly serious as it is.

the jury

before there is a police report
if there is a police report
before there is a trial
if there is a trial
before there is any attempt
at legal
justice

there is the jury

the jury
is the families and friends
the co-workers and classmates and acquaintances
the ungathered crowd
whose mixed reaction of support or disbelief
of accountability or failure to take responsibility
determines everything to come

the jury
is the difference between leaving abuse
and being forced/coerced/manipulated/shamed/guilted
into staying

the jury
is the difference between ending violence against the victim
and perpetrating even more violence against them

the jury
can be abusers too
the psychological abuse of disbelief
of victim-blame
of gossip-mongering
are gaslighting all over again
are doing the abuser's work

the jury
is the difference between life and death

for a while
the jury is everything

not because they make decisions
about the perpetrator

but because they lay down the law
the ultimate verdict
for the victim

the answer to the question
will anyone believe me?

the jury deliberates and decides

everyone else

they hide behind their awkwardness
as if our trauma
exists solely as an imposition on them
as if we were raped
just to make their social interactions more difficult
as if our abuse
was some sort of strategy
to complicate who they were Facebook friends with

sometimes
this is what remains with us the longest
not the monstrousness of our abusers
but the total absence of empathy
from everyone else

exorcism

the therapist asks me to imagine
people from my past
in turn
sitting on a chair
between us

my rapist and abuser
first
then the people who enabled and enforced
the abuse
through their complicity
their silence
their lack of empathy or support

I put each of them
in the chair
in turn
I remember
every detail
they are still so real

I tell them
what I need to say
what they need to understand
at the end of each conversation
I finish with the final words
you are dead to me

I do not wish violence upon you
I will not inflict it
will not do to you what you did to me
there are no excuses for that

you are dead to me

I have tried to forgive
and it doesn't help
doesn't liberate me
doesn't bring closure
only final words do that

you are dead to me

some I am furious with
some I feel sorry for
some I barely remember
but all are in the past now

you were dead to me
now you are nothing

ten things

ten things
people told me
when I reported my abuse

1. 'I don't want to pick sides'

2. 'I don't know
how to respond
hearing this is really hard
for me'

3. 'I don't understand
you need to convince me
by telling me
every traumatic detail
of what was done to you'

4. 'I don't want to believe
you're the kind of person
who would lie about this
but
I just don't know'

5. 'you should probably
talk to your rapist
about it
sort it out between yourselves'

6. 'that's not my problem'

7. 'I just don't believe
he would do
something like that'

8. 'I just don't know
if I believe you'

9. 'I don't believe you'

10. 'I don't believe you'

ten things
I needed
people to tell me
when I reported my abuse

(ten things
you *need*
to tell anyone
in your life
who tells you
about their abuse)

1. I am sorry *that* this happened to you

2. it wasn't your fault

3. you have nothing to apologise for

4. how can I help?

5. I will stand with you

6. is there something
I can do
to help keep you safe?

7. you can talk to me

8. I believe you

9. I believe you

10. I believe you

Friends And Family: We Need To Talk about your job from now on

Your loved one is going to need support. Is going to need care and nurturing. Is going to need space and autonomy to make their own decisions, while knowing that you have their backs when they do. Whatever they do. Whichever choices they make.

This is your job from now on. To be their support without them having to ask. To listen to what they need and respect their boundaries and decisions.

There are few jobs as important as that. Take pride in it.
And learn the craft of the work ahead of you.

I believe you

most rape
has nothing to do with walking home
or with night-time
or with strangers

most rape
is nothing like
the movies
or sex ed class
or freshman orientation

most rapes
are committed by people
you trust
by your partner
or family member
or friend
or date

most rapes are never reported
most rapes are never even spoken of

most people who are raped
never tell anyone
let that sink in
never tell anyone

never
tell
anyone

so if someone tells you
what happened to them
take them seriously
take their word for it
take on the job
of responding with care

start by obliterating their biggest fear
start with saying
'I believe you'

you don't need to know
what happened
not really

not in the clinical questions
asked by the hospital staff
or in the intrusive disbelief
of the police

you don't need to know
what was done to me
not how
or how often
not really

graphic detail will not make you
better able to support me
it will only make me
less able to support myself

let the police ask the questions
let the counsellor receive the answers
let the notebook take my memories

I do not need you to understand
no one who has not lived this can truly understand
so I hope you never do

I do not need you to understand
I need you to listen

listen to the things I don't have words for
listen to the silence that falls around me
when someone mentions my abuser's name

notice the way my muscles tense up
involuntarily
when someone jokes
about assault

listen to the way
sound scares me
movement scares me

touch scares me

notice the bags under my eyes
when the nightmares
have kept me up all night
every night

listen to the things I don't have words for

listen to the way I need you
need my family and my friends
need my support and my safety

I don't need you to understand

just be there
be here
without questions
without answers
without unsolicited advice
without the expectation
that I'll be 'back to normal' soon

this is my normal now
there is no going back
only going forward

so please
listen to the things I don't have words for

life or death

I wish I didn't know that pause so well
that pause after I tell them
after I tell them what's happened to me
what happened to me for years
and I wait

I wait in that pause
before they tell me they believe me
that they believe this really did happen to me

still
still after all this time
after all these years
that pause brings everything back
the telling of all those first people
who did not believe me
or did not think it serious enough to act
because
it was inconvenient to them
or because he was
such a good guy
he couldn't have
would never
because he was such a good guy
or he was an asshole
but he'd never
he'd never do that
would he
?

and in this pause it all comes flooding back
all that worry and insecurity
all that denial and doubt

if I speak
will I be believed?
if I am quiet
will it happen again
to someone else?
if I speak
will everything shatter
like he said it would?

if I speak
will no one believe me
?

still
after all this time
I cry after that pause
after telling
someone I have to work with
someone I have to live with
someone I have just met
someone I don't want to have to tell

I cannot choose silence over safety
comfort over clarity
I do not have the luxury of choosing

after all this time
that pause still gets me
it still gets me
every time

that feeling
that everything is on a knife's edge
and this person believing me
is still
still always
for a fraction of a moment

life or death

why they call us survivors

we are fighting
every day
can't you see it

we are
living
proof

after all
we are
still here

Everyone: We Need to Talk to Each Other

On how rape culture is created and can be changed.
On how consent is a conversation.
On the work ahead of us.

We Need To Talk To Each Other
listening to victims and survivors

It should go without saying that those who have experienced sexual violence know what they are talking about. And yet far too often, when political or legal decisions are made concerning violence and victims, we are spoken about, but not spoken to. Not heard.

When stories about sexual violence are told in newspapers and fiction, they are not the stories of the victim(s). They are not told on the victim's terms. In the victim's own time frame. For the victim's benefit. In ways that help the victim recover or stay safe.

And we are tired of being talked about, but never heard. If we are to end sexual violence and its prevalence (and believe me, we are), then we need to start by listening to victims and survivors.

they will say

they will say words like
brave
like *courageous*
like *role model*

they will call me things like
slut
like *feminazi*
like *liar*

they will say things like
exaggeration
like *selfish bitch*
like *anecdotal evidence*

they will
hate
and they will
praise
and they will
mute

they will attempt
to silence
to amplify
to respond
to critique
to hack
to reclaim
to distance, discuss, and dissent
they will –

but none of it matters now
because I have done
what I needed to do
I have told
the truth

our stories

these stories
belong to us
because we have lived them
they are not just statistics
not just the number of police reports
or rape crisis centre users
or phone calls to helplines

these stories are in our bodies
in our nervous systems
in our minds as we sleep
our muscles remember still
our fight-or-flight-or-freeze response
will be on the highest warning level
for the rest of our lives
and in our sleep
we are still there
still stuck
still never getting out alive

reclaiming our stories
is more than symbolic
more than political expression
more than gesture
it is owning ourselves again
belonging to ourselves again
existing on our own terms

trauma does not leave
although it dulls with time
the least you can do
is not inflict it again
by treating us
as numbers
as abstracts
as non-people

use numbers
if it helps with change
use stories
if it aids in understanding
be strategic and statistic
and political

but know
know always
that our stories
belong to us

abuse is a building
burning
invisibly

abuse is the floodgates
breached
but no one notices

abuse is a tree
being slowly chopped apart
for firewood

it is gradual
and instantly violent
it is the boiling of the frog
by increasing the temperature degree by degree

it is never as simple
as

why didn't you just leave?

watching the door

I grew tired of watching the door
everywhere I went
always in the back of my head
worried
my abuser would walk in

friends started asking
why do you always sit facing the door
in cafés
in pubs
in your own home?
why do you keep looking up
with every person who walks in?
who are you waiting for?

I didn't know what to tell them
except I was always on guard
was always watching
always waiting for the worst to happen
as it had
before
again
and again
and again

so now I kept a lookout
always ready
for whenever he walked in
again

I grew tired of watching doors
tired of shrinking into corners and silences
and so slowly
deliberately
painfully

I learned
to become visible again

now
I sit in windows
make myself mighty
make myself seen

book in hand
tea on side
alone except for my favourite company
– my own

I am no longer
hiding in corners
no longer terrified
watching the door

now
I take up space
make myself known
sit proudly
where I am clearly visible
send a silent message

I will not be frightened into silence

why I stayed

*(victims of abuse are asked again and again
'why didn't you just leave?'
this is how the hashtag #WhyIStayed began)*

#WhyIStayed
because I never thought of myself as abused
because I never considered what was done to me rape
because my abuser's truth always seemed more likely than mine
(I later learned this was called gaslighting)
because psychological abuse is a powerful tool
because denial is a persuasive voice in your head

because he threatened me
with what would happen if I left

because leaving abuse
is the most dangerous thing a victim can do
because the violence always gets worse
when you consider leaving
because the violence stops
for a while
when you decide to stay

because he told me again and again
that no one would believe me
and he was nearly right

because staying in abuse means continuing the narrative
that abuse could never happen to you
and that is a great story to tell yourself

because leaving abuse
means accepting what has been done to you
because denial is a cocoon
most people would choose
over being treated
the way victims of abuse are treated

because reporting abuse
is being retraumatised all over again
because not reporting abuse
feels like accepting you will never have justice

will never be believed
that your abuser was right

because leaving abuse meant leaving
not just my relationship
but my friends
my work
my daily life
everything I had worked so hard to build

because what happens after abuse
can be just as awful
as the abuse itself
because being doubted
because being interrogated
because being gossiped about
because having your emotional wound of trauma
studied and judged and rated for believability
by complete strangers
is only marginally better
than abuse

because leaving
is when your memories come back
when your PTSD kicks in
when you start fighting yourself
instead of your abuser

because it gets worse
before it gets better

because we treat victims
as if they are on trial
and perpetrators
as if they are victims of their own actions

we don't cry wolf

when someone goes stalking for prey
scans crowds with hungry eyes
shouts 'meat market'
slips something into a drink

we don't cry wolf

instead
we cry victim
we cry
why were you wearing that, victim?
we cry
what were you thinking
drinking like that, victim?
we cry
why would you walk home
alone
at night
'victim'?

we don't cry wolf
but how loudly we cry victim
gossip it to friends
sneer it in court
mock it in the news

hearing victim
cried so often
it starts to sound like blame
we learn to be blameless
learn to carry
pepper spray
keep police apps on our phone
call our friends as we walk home
there's a whole industry
dedicated to making us blameless
for crimes committed against us
of course anti-rape underwear
doesn't prevent rape
of course
nail polish that changes colour upon contact with date rape drugs
doesn't prevent rape
of course not

but in our desperation
we hope they keep us from being blamed
we hope they pass the Russian roulette from us
and on to
who?
someone else
anyone else
someone who wasn't as cautious

as if the problem is us
our risk-taking
our over-trusting
our naïveté
our lack of preparedness
or street smarts
or blamelessness

as if we didn't know
that there will always be a girl
who is drunker
who can't afford a taxi
whose friends aren't there to walk her home
whose phone is out of battery
who is simply
more vulnerable than us
more prey than us

as if we didn't know
that all of our preparedness
does not stop violence from happening
it simply passes it on
to her
passes on the attack
to her
the rape
to her
the victim blame
to her

as if we didn't know
that our preparedness
solves nothing
it just passes on

the symptoms of the problem
the blame of the problem
to another victim

we have cried
victim
enough now
it solves
nothing
saves
no one

it is time we talk about
who is responsible

it is time
we cried
perpetrator

We Need To Talk To Each Other about masculinity

While victims of sexual violence are of every gender, age, ethnicity, ability, nationality, sexuality, religion and class – one thing is certain. The absolute, overwhelming majority of perpetrators have one thing in common. They are men.

If we are to end sexual violence, and the particular stigma faced by male victims of rape and abuse, we need boys and men to start doing the work of changing masculinity. To talk about masculinity, consent and violence with other boys and men. To change norms from the inside. To end the idea that violent or aggressive behaviour is somehow appropriate or attractive or even necessary to be considered a 'real man'.

We need boys and men to talk to other boys and men about how to change masculinity. Many are already leading the way.

We need more of you.

you're so vain

    (to #notallmen)

you're so vain
you probably think
this book
is about you

when it was about
destructive masculinity
this whole time

why do rape apologists think men are animals?

it only matters what the victim wore
or how much they drank
or if they were flirting
or how many sexual partners they have had
if we believe men
are incapable of controlling themselves

honestly
how else could any of those questions matter
you cannot invite rape
unless rape is some sort of force of nature
unless men
are incapable
of not raping someone
once they've been turned on

it only matters what the victim was doing
if we believe perpetrators
are unable to make decisions about their own actions

as a man
don't you find it horrible
to be seen as an animal
by men's rights activists?

as a man
don't you find it offensive
that rape apologists
think you are so incapable of rational thought
of self-control
of basic human functioning
that you could rape someone
simply because you
'couldn't stop yourself'?

don't you believe
you are capable
of choosing your actions
of human communication
of understanding the difference between consenting sex and rape

(you know
the way feminists

believe you are fully human
rather than mindless animal)?

as a man
aren't you angry
that perpetrators
are getting away with this
with arguing
that you are all so controlled by your sex drive
that you become entirely blind and deaf
that you can't tell the difference
between a consenting partner
and someone who is fighting back
someone who is screaming no
someone who is frozen in fear
someone who is unconscious or asleep?

why aren't you
#notallmen-ing
the argument
that you cannot be held accountable for your own actions
because you are somehow
erectally incontinent
intellectually incompetent
somehow incapable
of choosing whether or not
you force yourself on other people?

why aren't you angry
rape apologists
believe so little of you

when the rest of us
think you are
capable
of so much?

# of monsters and men

let's get something straight
you know a rapist
statistically speaking
you likely know more than one

statistically speaking
you are friends with a rapist
statistically speaking
you are related to a rapist
statistically speaking
if you sleep with men
you have likely slept with a rapist

the fact that you have not
seen these people rape someone
or been raped by them
does not mean that they are not rapists

by statistics alone
so few people report their rape
or even speak about their rape
that you likely know a rapist
without knowing that they are one

you probably think this person is a good guy
you probably think this person
would never do anything to hurt anyone
it is entirely possible
that this is what the rapist thinks of himself as well

(because yes
while victims of sexual assault
are of every gender
the absolute majority of rapists
are men)

most rapists are not
however
monsters

by that I mean
most rapists are not
antisocial weirdos

who jump out of dark alleys at night
and attack their victims

in fact
most rapists know their victim
and maintain an image
before and after assaulting someone
that makes people believe that they never could have

because a rapist
can rape one person
and have consensual sex with others

because a rapist
can abuse one partner
and have been kind and caring to another

because being a rapist
is not a personality trait
is not a visible marker
is not an identity

and often
no one but the victim(s)
knows what the rapist is capable of

in short
rapists are not monsters
more often than not
they are
'stand-up guys'
they are
'pillars of the community'
they are
'family men'

this is the defence
used again and again
in courts
and newspapers
to excuse rapists' actions
and invalidate
victims' testimonies

but the fact is
rapists are not monsters
not to everyone
and not all the time

this does not invalidate
the fact
of their monstrous actions against their victim(s)

most rapists
seem like perfectly ordinary
men
maybe even particularly charming ones

just like all the rapists
you know
but aren't aware you do
yet

no one is born a rapist

no one
is born
a rapist
they are nurtured into one
raised into one
rape-joked
and slut-shamed
and I'd-hit-that into one

they are
cockblocked
and fucking friendzoned
and prickteased
and don't-start-what-you-can't-finish
into one

they are told
to be dominant
they are told
to be aggressive
they are told
that perseverance
is romantic
that not taking no for an answer
is sexy

they are told
they are pussies and fags
and whipped and virgins
if they don't

that if they don't
nag and guilt-trip
and force and claim
and manipulate and neg
and coerce and conquer
their way to sex
then they aren't
real men

no one is born a rapist
they are
boys-will-be-boys'd into one

porned into one
excused into one
normalised into one

they are
taught by example

in a never-ending class
taught through tradition
in every friend group
and classroom
and street

no one is born a rapist
but we are raising them

we
are raising them

an army of them
every new generation
our culture is fostering
rapist upon rapist
upon rapist
upon rapist
and we need
to stop

We Need To Talk To Each Other about consent

I think of consent culture as the opposite of rape culture. Consent culture is where it would be completely and absolutely normal to have conversations about sex, and desire, and safety. To have those conversations in schools and homes. And to have those conversations with anyone you would like to sleep with. Before you sleep together. Where if someone does not respect consent, that is immediately recognised, acknowledged and dealt with. Where if you reported rape, it would be taken extremely seriously. Where hopefully there would never be a rape to report.

Rape culture, meaning the entirety of the world we live in now, is the opposite of that. A world in which sexual violence is rampant and normalised. In which rape is used as a weapon of war and a system of punishment. In which sexual violence is a global epidemic.

Undoing rape culture requires having some important conversations about consent. That is why we need to talk.

state of emergency

when you declare a state of emergency
in a relationship
all rules are disbanded
you can crack down on dissent
undo consent
criminalise boundaries set by anyone but you

declaring a state of emergency
in a relationship
is how you make abuse possible

when you play the self-pity card
the jealousy card
the anger card
when you blame your anger and suspicion
on your terrible childhood
when you blame your drinking
on how much you work
when you blame your shouting
on your fear of being cheated on
when you blame your
unacceptable behaviour
on stress
on your mental health
on your misunderstood genius

you begin to move the boundaries of what is acceptable
begin to rationalise your hostile takeover
of another person

when you declare a state of emergency
in your relationship
you call it crisis
you call it temporary
you call it anyone's fault but your own
and slowly you take control
put your needs
on the official list of priorities
label the other person's needs
selfish
unpatriotic
unconstitutional
their needs

their emotions
become mere shadows
as you move borders
bend boundaries
break trusts

after all
your needs come first
after all
this is a state of emergency
and normal rules
no longer apply

you declare a state of emergency
because
you were drunk
or you felt attacked
or can't we see how overworked you are
or can't we cut you some slack
or who do we think we are
making demands of respect
from you
from *you*?
don't we know who you are?

and after a while
it doesn't matter if we protest
and anyway
we have stopped protesting
you have suspended the right to protest
it's for the greater good, you say
just for this transitional period
and anyway who are we to protest
to question your motives
to deem ourselves worthy of knowing your reasons?
we are selfish then
or unreliable
a liability
and don't we know no one else would love us?

we just don't understand the pressure you're under
the security concerns alone…

at this point
we are no longer people to you
no longer partners or loved ones
no longer citizens with rights
we are simply mirrors
to reflect back your greatness
we are simply crowds to shower you in glory
or if we refuse
or if we protest
we become enemies
of your state
alien combatants
that you will have to be tough with
tough love
you'll say
the only language they understand
you'll say
spare the rod
you'll say

there is a reason
soldiers, refugees and abuse survivors
are the most likely
to suffer from post-traumatic stress disorder
we are fighting a war here
only we are taken as prisoners
before we ever understand
a war has broken out
before we ever learn
to fight back

so what if we ended up in hospital?
this is a state of emergency
so what if we're exhausted or afraid?
what do we know about real hardship?
so what if you did hit us?
so what if we did say no?
scream it or fight back?
there are always losses in war
there are always casualties
can't we understand
ours is not to ask why?

this is a state of emergency after all
and we have become not loved ones
but national resources
yours to dispose of
we no longer own ourselves

we no longer own our bodies
they can be occupied at any time
called into dutiful service for the greater good
we should be grateful
you'll say
grateful we have a role to play here
should play it proudly
not protest
not cry
don't we understand
we are ruining this
for you?

who are we to deny?
to make demands?
to say no?
don't we know who you are?
and this is a state of emergency
after all
fights must be rationed
better to shut up and take it
better to offer willingly than to have it stolen
better to not provoke you
not to go to sleep angry
not make things harder for ourselves

you are under a lot of pressure
we must understand
this is a state of emergency
after all

this is the process
of overthrowing our autonomy
a state of emergency
is only ever a hostile takeover
by legitimate terms

and this is a state of emergency
after all
meaning we no longer
make the rules
of our own lives

speak

drunkenly
we fall out of clubs, pubs and ill-advised flat parties
fall into arms, clothes, bodies
loudly or wordlessly entangle our way into
ecstasy
sometimes
sometimes
we wake up feeling happy, bubbly, touchy, feely
ready to attach some more
ready to see where things could go

and sometimes
sometimes
we wake up perfectly and comfortably detached
feeling friendly, feeling free
saying goodbye amicably
never to intend to meet again

those are the great times
the times coloured by pleasure and desire
unmarked by awkwardness, shame, uncertainty, guilt
times that are sobering
as well as a little more drunk than we'd like to admit

but other times
other times
long nights of talking and silent looks of agreement
don't leave us enough words to speak
to say what we want
what we crave
what we are desperately needing
and those times
those times
there is something about the club beats
that beats us down
silences us
leaves our bodies vibrating
but our mouths lame
our thoughts uncommunicated

those times
those times when we are unable to form meetings
unshaped by the stereotype of

drunk casual sex
it is more important than ever
to step outside the box
and let us speak

speak because you deserve to know
that sex will be on your terms as well as theirs
speak
because you have a right
to feel safe and free and true to what you want
speak
because desire is meant to be easy

step out the box
and
speak
speak
speak

I never learned the words
never learned how to speak pleasure, consent, desire, preference
with men
but in queer clubs
I learned code
earrings, bracelets, pins and handkerchiefs
all told the stories
of things we were too awkward to say
and then there was the more complex stuff
flirting in the toilet queue, asking
'can I borrow a tampon'
code
meaning
I probably don't want sex tonight
but I'd like to take you home
see what else we can be with each other
or standing in the taxi queue, saying
'I've got an early morning, do you mind if we head to mine?'
code
meaning
I want sex
but might not be looking for intimacy
don't expect breakfast

in queer clubs
I learned to speak code
but code is not language
there is a limited number of things code can communicate
and our sexualities and preferences are not limited
they're endless, fluid, ever-changing
and code is not enough

I remember a boy
speaking the codes better than anyone
but unable to say what he meant
he'd roam the dance floors
his heart beating in Morse code
what his language
would not let him say
hold me
wishing desperately that he knew a way to ask
to ask that boy
the one in the corner
to take him home, hold him, and let him keep his clothes on
this asexual boy in this most sexualised place
with no words left to him

how do we communicate our drunken desires
fall into each other honestly and respectfully
when we don't have words?
the truth is
that we don't

so we must learn
how to speak
speak sex
like you have never been told it was ugly, dirty, shameful
speak desire
like you have never been told yours were wrong
speak consent joyfully
speak it like it matters
that you can look each other in the eyes in the morning
speak it like it matters
that you can look yourself in the mirror
and feel beautiful, truthful, whole
speak like you are trying to make friends as much as lovers
speak like you are trying to get to know yourself

as much as them
speak
speak
speak

because words are all we have
against the deafening sound
of club beats
speak

We Need To Talk To Each Other about how to reclaim the internet

When it comes to gender-based violence, the internet reflects and amplifies the offline world. There is an epidemic of gender-based violence online, with clear racist and transphobic parameters.

Not only is the relative anonymity of the internet used by strangers to harass and threaten public and semi-public figures; the internet has increasingly become a tool to exercise coercive control. To use threats and revenge porn and to continue abuse after a victim has left.

Largely, our laws do not cover online violence. Largely, police departments do nothing. Largely, social media corporations take no responsibility for violence perpetrated on their platforms.

The effect is a silencing of people. A further normalisation of violence. A removal of oppressed voices from online conversations. Because increasingly people fear being targeted by abuse if they speak. So they stay silent.

That's why we must reclaim the internet.

did you know

did you know
that nearly half of all women face harassment and abuse online?
that among women under thirty, that figure rises to 76%?
that a violent culture against women and trans people is by researchers considered 'established norm' online?

that online violence is clearly and measurably intersectional?

that people of colour face significantly more harassment and abuse than white people do online, with 32% of Asian people, 32% of Hispanic people, and 28% of black people reporting online harassment as compared to 23% of white people?
that 32% of LGBT youth report being sexually harassed online? that that is almost four times as much as straight, cis youth?

did you know
that online violence is actively silencing people and restricting their lives and participation?
that online violence is cited as the main reason teen girls do not participate in online activities as actively as they would like?

did you know
that online violence has economic costs for the victim?
that online violence has political costs for the victim, making them alter their offline behaviour – scared to attend certain events and to share their views both on- and offline?
that victims nearly always have to pay, for example for therapy, for self-defence classes, for home surveillance when online harassment turns into on- and offline stalking?

did you know
that female and trans public figures – journalists, YouTubers, athletes, actresses and artists – receive such sustained and continual harassment, abuse, rape and death threats online that many of them have to employ someone part- or full-time just to look through their social media feeds and report to the police?

did you know
that because the internet has no borders, it also often has no police departments and legal jurisdictions?
that there is no clear way to report to the police in the country where you live if the IP address of your abuser is in a different country?
that police departments across countries claim they are completely

overwhelmed with reports of online violence, and have almost no training, no resources and no laws to back up doing anything with the constant influx of reports?

did you know
that most victims of domestic abuse are also abused online, through surveillance apps and stalking on social media?
that this keeps victims from being able to leave domestic abuse, because their abusers continue the abuse online?
that one in ten intimate partners threatens an ex with revenge porn, or the non-consensual sharing of sexual images of their ex?
that two thirds of stalkers use online means to stalk their victims and 20% show up at their door with weapons?

did you know
that online abuse results in actual murders and real suicides?

did you know
that the UN considers online violence a major issue for girls and women worldwide?
that online gender-based violence is categorised in some legal systems as hate speech and against human rights?

did you know
that we have to start doing something
now
?

autocorrect

my phone keeps autosuggesting
my rapist's name

Twitter wonders if maybe I know my rapist

Facebook keeps trying to get me to befriend him

the police tell me
to forget

online violence

did you know that threats of violence
are neurologically experienced as violence?
I didn't

did you know that online abuse
can be just as traumatic as domestic abuse?
as a survivor of both
I guess I should have

but there is an idea
about online violence
that claims it's not *real*
that *online*
is opposite to *real world*
that
this is just the way the internet works

did you know that I continued to insist
that online violence didn't affect me
even as
waves of death threats and rape threats
triggered my PTSD?
time and time again
I would insist
that I was stronger than that
that I needed to be
stronger than that

that somehow
the only narrative
was victim or warrior
there was no place for vulnerable
no place for human
no place for real people
only for these caricatures

as if trolls
weren't people in your family
weren't your friends
weren't your co-workers and classmates
as if abusers were someone else
as if you didn't know a rapist

(I promise you
you do
probably a lot more than one)

and no
you can't tell from the outside
and no
you don't know until someone tells you
but then you do

then you know
and when you know
there is no room for doubt
for second-guessing the victim

so when I tell you
online threats of violence
are experienced in the same way
physical violence is
when I tell you
threats received online
result in trauma
I want you to know
that it is true
that it is real

and that the time is over
for talking about this
as unconnected
as unimportant
as not
In Real Life

just a click away

the early internet philosophers
imagined the online world
as one without discrimination
a place of total equality and trust

the early internet philosophers
imagined a place free from bodily identities
as gender, age, ability, ethnicity and nationality
were stripped away by binary code
they imagined what would remain
was
a utopia of sorts
a freedom
from oppression

pessimists say what we have now
the hatred
and threats
the Twitter storms
and trolls
that the internet we have now
shows the innermost
purest and ugliest
form of humanity
what we have always been

pessimists say that the internet
holds up a mirror to what it is to be human
shows us what we always were
only now
that we can be
(somewhat)
anonymous

we let it out

I think they're all wrong
the philosophers and the pessimists alike
the internet is neither utopia nor dystopia
like any other place
it is a living breathing thing
a culture we create and recreate
with every click

with every type
with every view and retweet and like

just as in the rest of our world
individual people can corrupt
places and politics and discourses
groups of people can render
the unacceptable normal
and the violent everyday

so war is made
and oppression is made
and so
the darkest corners of the internet
are made and made again

but just as war and oppression
just as threats and violence
are made
they can be
unmade
remade
changed

maybe we won't have utopia online
maybe the early philosophers were wrong
but then so were the pessimists
because just as there is good in the world
just as there is light and hope
and kindness and care
just as there is resistance and change
outside the world of zeros and ones
so there is inside it

we choose
how an internet of tomorrow
will look
and it is
only a click
away

#reclaimtheinternet

(first published in collaboration with the Dangerous Women Project)

to speak while woman
write while woman
exist online while woman
is dangerous

there is an online epidemic
of violence against women

don't believe me?
ask any woman who writes online
any female gamer or sports commentator
any journalist or artist
and you will find a backlog
of death threat upon death threat
upon rape threat upon rape threat
always rape threats

how did it come to this?

to generations of terrified men
hiding behind screens
muttering violent utterings
whore
slut
cunt
feminazi
?

why are they so afraid
of what we have to say
that every time I post a new poem online
I will inevitably get the comment
shut the fuck up
?

to be dangerous
is to speak while woman
to speak truth to power
to speak truth to power
to speak at all
while woman
is dangerous

because when we decide to speak
we become dangerous women
when we decide to speak
we become dangerous to the status quo
because our voices can shatter glass ceilings
because our words can tear apart silences
woven shut over centuries
because for us to be heard
instead of just seen
is still
revolutionary

when I speak online
about women's rights to their own bodies
terrified little men threaten to hang me from trees
to rape me out of my opinion
to force me to stay silent
to force me to shut up

to become a dangerous woman
is to choose to be heard
instead of just seen
is to decide that your favourite body part
is not
your tits
or your ass
or your waist
but your teeth
your tongue
your vocal cords
it's to find that the most beautiful part of yourself
cannot be seen by outsiders
because it resides within your mind

every time I receive a wave of online violence and abuse
I find it is the same thing
it is always from men
it is only from men
and it is never about
what I am speaking about

it is about the fact that I am speaking
that I dare to be speaking

while living in this body
while this body is living in this world

the first time
I received a death threat for my poetry
I was proud
I belly-laughed with the joy of it
I wore it as a badge of honour
and I felt it read
I AM A DANGEROUS WOMAN
I THREATEN PATRIARCHY
I MAKE THE STATUS QUO
SHAKE TO ITS CORE
I AM A DANGEROUS WOMAN
HEAR ME ROAR

the first time
I received a death threat online
I was proud
I had made some little man so afraid
he used every word he had ever learned
to shut a woman down
to silence and disbelieve
to force us into quiet
whore
slut
cunt
feminazi

the first time
I received a death threat
for one of my poems
I was proud
but the tenth time
the eleventh time
the twelfth time
I received a death threat
for one of my poems
I was tired
I was annoyed
I was exhausted
I was furious

I am not the only woman facing this
many have it far worse online than I do

how many more?
how many more women threatened with murder
for speaking
before we act up?
how many more
before we reclaim the internet
as we reclaim our streets?
how many more men
and young boys
socialised into misogyny
behind anonymous screens?

this isn't helping men either
you know that
right?
I receive letters of support from men
every week
men who are exhausted and struggling and terrified
of trying to live up to the expectations of being a
'real man'
men who are angry
with the violence they see directed at women
men who are exhausted
not knowing how to end that violence
not knowing what to do

this is not about individual men
and it's not about a few internet trolls either
this is not about all men
or some men
this is about masculinity

this is about masculinity
gone toxic and afraid
this is about masculinity
gone violent
this is about a system of patriarchy
so afraid of what we have to say
and the fact that anyone can hear us say it
that it will threaten us

that it will abuse us and harass us
that it will use the only tools
it knows how
more patriarchy
more death threats
more rape threats

and you might not see it
but patriarchy is failing
patriarchy is stumbling and falling
you might not see it
but patriarchy is losing
it is its dying breath
and it's using it to deny
how badly it's going

it's patriarchy's dying breath
and it intends to go out fighting
to claw its way into the hearts of young men
who are so afraid of what their role will be
in a big bad world
that no longer belongs
to *only* them
but to all of us

whore
slut
cunt
feminazi

these are words used
to pin us down
to keep us quiet

but we are dangerous women
when we choose to speak

to choose to speak is to realise
that you
you are explosions
placed in the centre of the status quo
they are only looking for ways to disarm you
they are only looking for ways to silence you

to make you safe for them
to make you compliant

and they will not succeed

because we are dangerous women
because to speak
is to be a dangerous woman
and we
will
never
shut up

Everyone:
We Need to Start Doing

On what happens after we talk.
On what's next.
On how to change everything.

We Need To Start Doing what's next

I have spent a lot of time thinking about what the purpose of this book is, what I want it to lead to. I hope that it leads us to talk and listen. Part of the solution is to make people aware of the problem and our silent complicity in it. Our role in changing it. And we need to talk about that.

Rape jokes, homophobic, racist and transphobic jokes are part of what normalises sexual and gender-based violence. And we need to talk about that.

Myths and faulty narratives about rape and abuse are part of what keeps victims from accessing support, acknowledgement and justice. And we need to talk about that.

But the fact that we need to talk does not mean that the entire solution consists of us talking. Trust me, it doesn't.

So now that we've talked, let's think about what comes next. Because words are powerful, but we need more than words to end structural gender-based violence and sexual violence.

So let's start doing.

we know where we stand

they can shout and threaten
or respond with total silence
act like
they had no part in this
like this isn't their problem
their fault
their fight

like rape is a natural force
an accident without intention and action
– someone slipped and fell, that's all –

you and I
will still know
what those words mean
know the truth
behind those inactions
the loud message
of total silence
while we bleed

because we know what it takes
to break it all
by speaking it out
because we know the price
of truth

and we know where we stand

while they dance around the problem
point fingers
and issue blame

we know where we stand

in the centre of it all
arm in arm
with every other survivor
every victim who lived to tell the tale

we know where we stand

it's time for the rapists' shift

it is the rapists' turn
to be afraid now
we have done our shift

we have taken more
than anyone's fair share
of questions about
what exactly happened
and what were we wearing
and had we been drinking
and how could they know
we weren't making it all up

we have
earned the title *survivor*
let the rapists be afraid from now on
let them question themselves and their actions
let them confess to their mothers
let them cry in front of the police
be asked by strangers if what they heard was true
have anxiety attacks in public bathrooms
stare numbly at the doors of cafés
afraid we might walk in

we have already been through hell
been through rape and abuse
and terror
we have already
waded through denial
faced our fears
battled misconceptions
been failed by legal systems
we have already fought
to survive

it's their turn
to face the music
our shift is up
theirs is only starting

the future

(first published in collaboration with Roundhouse Theatre and BBC 1Extra)

I've seen the past
and I don't think I like him

I mean he is ugly
all weather-worn
and leather-wrinkled
all silver-lined
and rose-tinted

but he hides claws
under his cloak
and if he gets close enough
he will hook onto you
and never unclasp

I've seen the past
and so have you
he keeps calling us names
names like *suit* and *yourself*
names like *victim* and *blame*

he keeps muttering under his breath
words like *sexual* and *assault*
words like *domestic* and *abuse*
he stands on street corners
mumbling statistics
as if they were Cluedo clues
one in three women
by someone they trusted
in every house
behind every door

and he is
always right

I've seen the past
and I don't think I like him
so I'm leaving him behind

see, lately
lately I've seen the present
and I think I like her

she's all kind eyes and warm smiles
and she sings in the shower
songs of how there'll be days
to follow the mornings after
how light will break through yonder window
in police stations and courtrooms too
how people once called broken
will also have their dreams come true

and her songs are hopeful

I've seen the present
and she makes the past look
like the sham he is

he doesn't define us
she says
and this
this too
shall pass

I've seen the present
and she's so generous
she just keeps giving and giving
even when I don't dare to ask
she still makes it her task
to hand me
breath
upon breath
upon breath
this endless string of new beginnings
for us to joyfully accept

I've seen the present
but lately I've glimpsed her fairer sibling
the future

and
they
are
beautiful

the future
has more sparkle in their eye

than the open ocean on a sunny day
and their laughter is clear and pure

the past keeps throwing words at them
keeps catcalling them
broken and *unreal*
but the future
they just turn on their heel
and laugh at him
then walk onwards and away

as if to say
we have things to do
you and I
things to do
and worlds to change
and people to become
and words like
victim
cannot contain us

I've seen the future
and I think I love them

because they'll tell me
the broken courts
cannot define our truths
we will write our own stories
and the endings will belong to us alone

I've seen the future
and they're all open skies
and uncharted horizons
all days to come
and revolutions
we haven't even dared dream

I have seen
the future

I think
I'm even starting
to believe
they're real

"it gets better"

the violence doesn't end
when my nightmares stop
we don't close the door
on structural gender-based violence
the day I have my final therapy session

the salience of rape
as a weapon of war and oppression
of maintaining a patriarchical
white supremacist
cis-sexist
status quo
does not somehow finish
the day I stop searching
for my abuser's face
in crowded rooms

my trauma
and our allowance of structural sexual violence
cannot be separated

so don't you dare
talk to me about
'it gets better'
unless you're
standing on the barricades
walking in the marches
lobbying for the laws
and
changing things
for the better

We Need To Start Doing the final chapter: how to change everything

Now that we've talked, there's work to be done. Important and difficult and necessary work.

Holding people accountable, in your life, in your community, in your work or hobby or school, is hugely important.

And so is changing policy. Many refuges and support services for survivors of sexual violence either do not take in all victims or are being forced to close from underfunding. The result is the deaths of actual, real people who might otherwise have lived.

The problem is economic, is legal, is political. Is deeply ingrained. It is in the legislation on sexual violence and gender-based violence. It is in the legal institutions and police force. It is in our media and our classrooms and our homes.

We need to change attitudes and norms.
We need to change laws and how they are implemented.
We need to change ourselves and others.

In short, we need to change the world.

These are first steps, the beginning of an unfinished guide on

HOW TO CHANGE EVERYTHING.

we need to talk

I need to talk to you
about victims
I need to talk to you
as a victim
not because my story
is particularly unique
but because it isn't
because it is
disturbingly
violently
common

I need to talk to you
not for sympathy
or moral superiority
or political gain
not to place blame
on you
but because
we
as victims
are so often
talked about
and so rarely spoken to
listened to
heard

because rumour-spreading
and victim-blaming
and gaslighting
are weapons used against us

because anything
that causes disruption to the status quo
is dismissed through disbelief
so that when someone
(a victim)
challenges the way we like to see things
(normality)
and the way we like to think of people
(perpetrators)
they will be dismissed
any evidence will be rejected
because it leaves people
(the majority)

uncomfortable
and discomfort
in acknowledging violence
literally
kills

I want to talk to you
as a victim
because entire sets of laws
and police forces
and justice systems
are built around making
justice
safe for our perpetrators
(allegations, nothing's been proven, the rape kit came in too late, you know what jealous exes will do, that's just to get the money, the 'alleged' victim, only doing it for attention)
and impossible
for us

I want to talk to you
about victims
because psychological abuse by our perpetrators
(denying violence has ever occurred)
is often continued, enabled and enforced
by friends, family and strangers
(disbelieving or downplaying the existence or extent of violence)
and is continued in the interrogation practices
of police reports
and courtrooms
(putting the victim, their life and their sexual history on trial
innocent until proven guilty
seems only true
of the perpetrator)

and so a culture
of enabling and enforcing
the perpetrator's abuse on the victim
is continued
by the justice system
by the police departments
and often
by well-meaning people like you
often unconsciously and unreflectively
often seemingly innocent

and so a culture
of victim-blaming
a culture of excusing and belittling sexual violence
is reproduced
and reproduced
and reproduced

and so victims
are retraumatised
and retraumatised
and retraumatised

I want to talk to you
about victims
as a victim
because so often
the violence done to us
is seen as unconnected instances
never parts of the same puzzle
never points in the same structure
never symptoms of the same underlying disease

I want to talk to you
about victims
as a victim
because
what we know
should be common knowledge

because so often
we are only stories
someone else tells in warning
never stories we ourselves
get to choose when and how to tell

because
we have been quiet
long enough
and the silence
is killing us

we have been quiet
long enough
and it's time
finally
that we speak

self-help to revolt

I don't want self-help books
I want a step-by-step guide to social change
I want a DIY manual for survivors to revolt
I want us to self-help our way into a fucking revolution

people keep telling me
I'll get back to normal
eventually

get back to
normal
after the violence
only I don't want to go back to normal

'normal'
is one in two trans and non-binary people being assaulted
is one in three women being abused
is one in five men being subjected to sexual violence
is one in five children being forced to spend their lives coping with
the aftershocks of trauma

and I have to tell you
that no amount of
proper sleep and green vegetables
no amount of
healthy exercise and plenty of liquids
no amount of self-help
will change that
will make that OK
will make a dent
in the iceberg
of that trauma

so no
I don't want to go back to normal
I want to be angrier
than I ever was before
and I want you
to be angry with me

I am not looking for normalcy
after violence
I am looking for

some truly subversive
gender-radical
revolution
right about now

and I am telling you this
because my trauma
isn't private
isn't something you quietly
self-help your way out of

our traumas are political
our traumas are the result of politics
our traumas require political change

our traumas are political
and it is about time
you listened up
and started doing something

this movement

there is power in this movement
there is strength in our voices
there is might in our numbers

what we have is a movement
and don't underestimate
what a movement is capable of

for so long
I've been afraid
that this development
of racist
sexist
Nazi
fascist
populist
right-wing
corporatist
alt-right
upper-class white male
supremacy
is inevitable

that we
we
the alternative

we
the people
we
the uninvolved opinionators
have grown too comfortable
with what we have
to fight for change
to fight even
to keep
the limited rights
we have now

I have worried
for a long time
I have worried
that politics of fear

that hatemongers
and internet trolls
and terrifying politicians
will frighten us into apathy
and that that
will be the end
of democracy
as we know it

because it's happened before
and we are hella self-congratulatory
if we think
it can't happen to us

but the thing is
that I was wrong
I know now
that I was wrong
that anyone who spoke of the end of history
in neoliberalism
and the inevitability
of global capitalism
turning into corporate fascism
is wrong

it is not inevitable

we have already proven them wrong
because there is power in this movement
there is strength in our voices
there is might in our numbers
what we have is a movement
what we are
is a movement

and this goes so much further
than President Trump
so much further
than a single individual
and a single country
this is about an era
and an era
coming to a close

we have proven
we are strong
we have proven
that when we organise
we can make anything happen
we have proven
we can make real change come about

so come all ye
marchers and protesters
all ye tweeters and vloggers
come all ye
furious and exhausted
come all ye
hopeful and fighting
come
and let us build something better
let us build something else
let us build
an alternative
a movement
a change

we are capable of
this
of building
a feminist
anti-racist
pro-migrant
pro-Muslim
disability-inclusive
inter-faith
all genders
class-conscious
queer as fuck
movement

we are capable
of building the future

you and me
and everyone else
who believes in this

we can build this
movement
so let's start
together
let's start
right now

how to change everything

start with yourself
with learning
with reflecting
with examining your attitudes
your behaviours
how experiences
might differ from yours

move outwards
speak to those around you
ask questions
listen
reflect
propose change
propose togetherness

team up
think big
read up

there is more than individual experience
more than statistics and facts
there is plenty to learn
if you're willing
to listen
to read
to learn

make it a journey
make it a mission
make it worthwhile

learn about the laws
the police practices
the histories of violence
written on our bodies

join arms
let those who have lived through
march first
but join in the second rank
follow their lead
amplify their voices

build on their movement
enter their strategy
add to their strength

make a plan
make a change
make a difference

and change
everything

Bonus Section
Victims and Survivors: We Need to Write

On writing as therapy.
On breaking the silence.
On reclaiming our stories.

Victims And Survivors: We Need To Write
why write?

For me, choosing to write my story (for a long time, only in my diary and with no plan to show it to anyone) felt like taking back control over my life.

For me, it felt like reclaiming something that was stolen from me in the aftermath of trauma. For me, it felt like victory and revenge and therapy and blossoming and revolution.

For me, it felt like this book was the final step on a twisting and turning path I had been walking for years.

Maybe you are at a place in yourself and your recovery where writing could feel like some of those things to you too. If you are, the writing exercises in the end of this book are things I've written just for you.

Try them.

writing as therapy

when the world gets too much
when memories overwhelm me
or fears block my sight
I put pen to paper
put heart in hand
and I write

why write poems

(when there is so much important work to do)

I write my way
to safety
it is how I come home
to myself

Victims And Survivors: We Need To Write
writing exercises

You need to tell your own story.
On your own terms.
In your own time.

This is a series of writing exercises to help you along the way
to healing
to living
to revolution
to a future where violence plays no part.

I have invented these exercises. I have borrowed from mental health research and meditation techniques and arts therapy practices and personal experience. I have crafted them from hundreds of hours spent leading creative writing workshops and thousands of hours spent recovering from trauma.

I am offering them to you. If they are helpful, feel free to try them. If you find what you write is too heavy for you to bear, get in touch with me. I will gladly hold your story while you recover.

I'll see you in the circle.
At the end of the tunnel.
Where our words meet.

With love and solidarity,

rules for the writing exercises

These exercises are not about producing the most brilliant piece of writing anyone has ever written. Rather, they are a way to self-care, to cope and to imagine a life after violence.

As such, perfectionism, performance anxiety and self-doubt are potential demons you might have to slay along the way. Trying to write perfectly and beautifully and without spelling errors is a hindrance, not a help. So try to leave those concerns behind, and find the joy in creating instead.

RULES FOR ALL WRITING EXERCISES:
- don't judge what you write
- don't change what you write while writing it
- try not to worry about anything other than putting one word after the other, without pause and without hesitation
- if you at any point feel overwhelmed by triggers or trauma, stop and self-care
- your well-being matters. if writing helps in healing, write. if it doesn't right now, don't worry about it; pick it up another time

how to survive:
a writing exercise

NEED:
- something to write with
- something to write on
- a timer (for example your phone)
- an avoidance of distractions (set your phone to flight mode, turn off your internet)

1) At the top of your page, write:
HOW TO SURVIVE

2) Set your timer to four minutes. From when the timer starts to when the timer stops, just keep writing. Don't worry about spelling or grammar, good or bad. Just write.

3) Write a how-to guide for how to survive. For yourself. You already know how. Just remind yourself a little.

4) When the timer goes off, stop writing.

You did it. You are surviving. And I know that is not an easy thing to do.

space to write:

space to write:

letter to my future self having a rough time: a writing exercise

(inspired by Sophie Labelle's comic Assigned Male*)*

NEED:
- something to write with
- something to write on
- a timer (for example your phone)
- an avoidance of distractions (set your phone to flight mode, turn off your internet)

1) Set your timer to five minutes.

2) At the top of your page, write:
Dear future self having a rough time

3) Start your timer and fill your letter with support, advice, jokes – whatever comes to mind and might cheer you up when things feel really rough. You know better than anyone what you might need, want and appreciate.

4) Fold up your letter and save it for a rainy day.

5) If or when things feel rough, open the letter. Thank yourself. Write another letter.

Well done for supporting your future self. That is pretty cool of you.

space to write:

space to write:

what I need now: a writing exercise

NEED:
- something to write with
- something to write on
- a timer (for example your phone)
- an avoidance of distractions (set your phone to flight mode, turn off your internet)

This exercise is like a recipe. The final text is both a poem and a guide – for yourself and, if you like, for your loved ones.

Don't worry about it being good. Just write the first thing that comes to mind. And take care of yourself.

1) List your ingredients.

- What I need from myself
- What I need from the people around me
- What I need from the world

2) Write your instructions.

- How I will go about adding these things to my life
- Backup plan: if an ingredient is missing, what do I do?

3) You just finished your recipe of communicated needs. You know what you need. Now go get it, and ask for whatever help you require along the way. You deserve support and love and care.

space to write:

space to write:

letter to my younger self: a writing exercise

NEED:
- something to write with
- something to write on
- a timer (for example your phone)
- an avoidance of distractions (set your phone to flight mode, turn off your internet)

Sometimes, if we have been traumatised in adulthood or late childhood, we experience a sense of breakage, of being someone broken or fundamentally unlike the person we were before violence. It can help to talk to the person you were before, to forgive yourself for everything that has happened since. To redraw the line between who you were before and who you will be after. To connect.

1) On the top of your page, write:
LETTER TO MY YOUNGER SELF

You can choose a particular age or moment or have an open idea about what stage in your life you are speaking to yourself in.

2) Set your timer to six minutes.

3) Once you've started your timer, write a letter to yourself with all the advice, questions, knowledge and forgiveness you have now.

During this time, write and do not stop writing. If you feel triggered or unsafe, you should stop right away. But if you want to stop because you're worried the writing isn't good enough, just keep going. You are more than good enough.

If you want, finish with the final line:
you are not broken, I am still you

4) When the timer goes off, stop writing.

Forgive yourself for any unkind thoughts you had towards yourself, and for however hard or easy this was to do.

You just wrote a poem! Well done. I am proud of you.

space to write:

space to write:

mapping your way forward: a writing exercise

(based on the poem 'Provincialising Violence', under 'Victims and Survivors: We Need to Talk')

NEED:
- something to write with
- something to write on
- a timer (for example your phone)
- an avoidance of distractions (set your phone to flight mode, turn off your internet)

In this exercise, I will ask you to imagine your recovery as a path on a map. To imagine your life in visuals. If you want, you can draw this exercise instead of writing it. If you want, you can both write and draw. If you struggle to make sense of some of the instructions, fill in the gaps yourself or move on to the next part.

1) Imagine your life as a map.

Start with the centre of who you are, what is important to you, what you are good at, what you care about or are interested in. This is your capital, and the centre of your map.

2) Set your timer to three minutes

Spend these three minutes describing your capital – what is most important to you and who you are? What values, experiences, dreams? There is no wrong answer; just go with your gut.

When the timer goes off, no matter how finished or unfinished things feel, move on to the next step.

3) Set your timer to three minutes.

Write about the journey as you walk away from your imagined capital (yourself) and into the surrounding areas, where things that you love and hold dear are. What people are important to you? What places? What activities? Describe or draw them.

When your timer goes off, no matter how empty or full your page is, move on to the next step. Don't judge what you have made.

4) Set your timer to two minutes.

Imagine walking further out from the centre of you and towards the edges of your map. Write about or draw people and places that once mattered to you, but now matter less. Perhaps on your walk from the centre you walk past your primary school. Or somewhere you went once many years ago, but have never particularly wanted to go back to. Place your difficult experiences here, your traumas or heavy burdens. You do not need to describe them; just place them on your imaginary map and keep going.

When the timer goes off, move on to the next step.

5) Set your timer to one minute.

Work your way out to the very outskirts of yourself, the corners of your map. Describe or draw the line where you end and the world around you begins. Then stop writing.

Whatever you wrote or drew, you have mapped your life as it feels right now. That is enough. That is plenty. In a few weeks, or a few months, try repeating the exercise and notice how things have changed. How much further out on your map violence is by then. How much you are always building and rebuilding yourself from the core. Celebrate that.

space to write:

space to write:

imagining the future: a writing exercise

NEED:
- something to write with
- something to write on
- a timer (for example your phone)
- an avoidance of distractions (set your phone to flight mode, turn off your internet)

1) On the top of your page, write:
MY LIFE WILL BE…

In the middle of your page, write:
MY CHOICES WILL BE…

On the next-to-last line of your page, write:
MY WORLD WILL BE…

2) Set your timer to six minutes.

From when the timer starts to when it goes off, fill in the blank spaces on your page. Finish the sentences and connect the words between them. Write whatever comes to mind. Finish the last line.

3) When the timer goes off, stop writing.

You just wrote a poem (and predicted the future).

When things feel rough, look at this and remind yourself of what all this hard work is for. Remember this is where you're going.

space to write:

space to write:

reclaiming the story: a writing exercise

NEED:
- a black marker pen
- a newspaper article about rape or abuse
- a day when you feel good and full of anger

This exercise is only for days when you are doing well, mental health-wise, and feel able to accept that doing this will make you really angry. This exercise is for days when anger is your fuel, and when it helps you to keep going.

1) Take the newspaper article about rape or abuse. Take a black marker pen. Use the pen to black out all words that you do not need. Leave words unmarked by your pen to tell a new story.

Retell the story so that the victim has agency.
Retell the story in a way that feels fair to you.
Retell the story with anger or humour or hope.

Reclaim the story from ignorance.

2) When you have done this, give yourself a pat on the back.

Give yourself a treat.

And give yourself permission to do the same thing with your own story. Reclaim it.

space to write:

space to write:

how to change everything: a writing exercise

NEED:
- something to write with
- something to write on
- a belief that things can change

1) At the top of your page, write:
HOW TO CHANGE EVERYTHING

2) Set your timer to four minutes.

Write a how-to guide for how to CHANGE EVERYTHING. For yourself. Or the world. Or the people who come after you on this path. It doesn't have to be a perfect plan. It doesn't have to make sense. Or be spelled right. It just has to be.

4) When the timer goes off, stop writing.

When the timer goes off, start CHANGING EVERYTHING.

I'll be there right by your side.

space to write

space to write

space to write

space to write

space to write

space to write

space to write

space to write

space to write

space to write

More To Do

more to do

If you are a person with disposable income, please donate to some of the charities and shelters that allow victims to leave abuse and make support services for victims and survivors possible. Most are deeply under-resourced and do incredibly important work in keeping victims alive and safe and recovering.

If you are a victim or survivor in need of support, there are support services in your area that can offer shelter, counselling or legal support. Please turn to them. You deserve support and help in getting back on your feet.

The next pages include resources for learning more and accessing support services. Websites that offer support via chat, helplines that offer counsel via phone, and a variety of free online resources that can help in understanding, in keeping safe, in getting through, and in changing everything. Please don't hesitate to ask for support.

more to read

If you are interested in these topics and want to learn more, or if you need support services, there are many free resources available online. The specifics of legal support (and criminal justice systems) differ from country to country. But information and resources, as well as online support services for survivors, friends and family, can be helpful regardless of where you live.

Here are some good places to start.

reading tips for everyone

Recl@im the Internet
www.reclaimtheinternet.com
Campaign and resources for ending online violence.
Organisation and campaign to stop online abuse including threats, misogyny, racism, homophobia and intimidation. A place to actively take part, sign the petition and join in.

UNFPA (United Nations Population Fund)
www.unfpa.org/gender-based-violence
Helpful for understanding sexual violence as a weapon of war and a mechanism of systematic oppression.
Formal academic and political reports on the use of gender-based violence and sexual violence worldwide. Facts and statistics, as well as an overview to understanding the extent of the issue.

UN Women (United Nations)
www.unwomen.org/en/what-we-do/ending-violence-against-women
Helpful for understanding the big picture and the political nature of gender-based violence worldwide.
Sadly, as many of the resources available, mostly focused on violence against women, rather than gender-based violence and sexual violence against people of all genders. Still an incredibly helpful resource for understanding the global picture.

WMC Speech Project (Women's Media Center)
www.wmcspeechproject.com
Very useful guide to understanding online violence and abuse.
Offers a series of free helpful resources, including facts and statistics and the aptly titled 'Online Abuse 101', a guide to understanding important terms in online violence such as cyberexploitation or revenge porn, deadnaming, doxing, flaming, grooming, stalking by proxy, swatting and online abuse.

White Ribbon
www.whiteribbon.org.au/understand-domestic-violence
Resources and definitions for understanding domestic violence and different forms of abuse.
Clearly defines different types of abuse including physical abuse, financial abuse, emotional abuse, verbal abuse, social abuse, sexual abuse, stalking and spiritual abuse. Includes guides on key terms such as the cycle of abuse, domestic violence and family violence.

resources for victims and survivors and their friends and family

Angelou Centre
www.angelou-centre.org.uk
Support and information for female black and minority ethnic victims and survivors of sexual violence.
Information and resources provided by and for black and minority ethnic women victims and survivors.
Specific resources for female victims with disabilities.
Specific resources for LGBTQI+ victims.

LGBT Foundation
www.lgbt.foundation/information-advice/sexual-violence
Support and information specifically for trans, non-binary, intersex, lesbian, gay and bisexual survivors of sexual violence.
Free and downloadable guides on how to cope after sexual violence, the specific resources and support systems available, and the particular myths and misconceptions that LGBTQI+ survivors face.

RAINN (Rape, Abuse & Incest National Network)
www.rainn.org
Support services and resources for sexual violence survivors, including male survivors and childhood sexual abuse survivors.
Information, guides, helpline and chat support for sexual violence victims and survivors of all ages and genders.
Information in English and Spanish.
Specific resources for male survivors of sexual violence and the particular myths and misconceptions male victims face.
Specific resources for child and adult survivors of childhood sexual abuse and their loved ones.

Rape Crisis Scotland

www.rapecrisisscotland.org.uk/publications
Extremely helpful resources for victims and survivors, as well as for friends, family, partners and peers.
The website offers free online leaflets with information for victims on specific issues like trauma, sleep problems, self-harm, suicide, flashbacks, coping, healing, relationships and sexual health, to name just a few.

Specific resources for LGBTQI+ survivors.
Specific resources for survivors of childhood sexual abuse.
Online information specifically for friends, for partners, for parents and for peers of victims and survivors.

Shakti Women's Aid

www.shaktiedinburgh.co.uk
Helpline and online support for black and minority ethnic survivors of sexual violence in Arabic, Hindi, Mandarin, Polish, Portuguese, Punjabi, Spanish, Swahili, Urdu and English.
Support services in multiple languages. Information on domestic abuse including physical violence, psychological abuse, forced marriage, female genital mutilation and sexual violence.
Safe site to use if you are still living in an abusive household, as it covers online footprints.

final tips from the author

Find your own information. In other words: Google it.

There are lots of helpful online articles about how to end rape culture and implement consent culture.

There are talking points and resources for men and boys to challenge 'locker room talk' and to change masculinity for the better.

There are resources, information and advice specific to your area and your language, if your first language isn't English.

There are policy documents and formal rules and community guidelines about dealing with sexual violence and holding perpetrators accountable within your communities, within schools and workplaces and friend groups.

There is information and help to find. Use it.

finally:

There is work to be done.
So close the book.
And go out and
change everything.

thank you

to friends and family for getting me through
to domestic abuse and counselling services for life-saving support
to everyone dedicated to ending sexual and gender-based violence

to my publisher Burning Eye
to Jenn and Clive and Harriet and Liv
for having my back
and making this book happen

to every victim and survivor who stands before me
and each that comes after me
this is for us

to you
dear reader
for your future help in
changing everything

With love and solidarity,

Agnes

www.patreon.com/AgnesTorokPoet
www.agnestorok.org

Milton Keynes UK
Ingram Content Group UK Ltd.
UKHW022306170823
427054UK00011B/757